PRAISE FOR *GRAD SCHOOL ESSENTIALS*

"This witty and highly readable book smartly cuts through the mysteries of higher education and reduces them to clear, manageable steps. *Grad School Essentials* is a useful book for graduate students everywhere."

Barbie Zelizer, Raymond Williams Professor of Communication and Director, Annenberg Scholars Program in Culture and Communication, University of Pennsylvania

"This down-to-earth, accessible guide offers extremely valuable insights into reading, writing, and the often-ignored topic of students' academic demeanor. Every time I teach a course for undergraduates or graduates, I face students who struggle to perform the tasks that this book addresses. At last I can refer them to a resource they can truly use. I wish that all my students would assimilate the lessons Zachary Shore provides."

Michael Hechter, Foundation Professor of Political Science, Arizona State University, and Professor of Sociology, University of Copenhagen

"Zachary Shore has written a remarkably helpful guide to the crucial skills that students need as they navigate their way through undergraduate and graduate school. With catchy phrases and easy-to-remember guidelines, Shore speaks to the student in his own distinctive voice. Shore is himself a phenomenon, zipping through graduate school at challenging institutions, discovering neglected archives, writing five books, and accumulating a host of awards and fellowships. His many successes give him the authority to write a book of this kind."

Arlene Saxonhouse, Professor of Political Science and Women's Studies, University of Michigan

Grad School Essentials

Grad School Essentials

A Crash Course in Scholarly Skills

Zachary Shore

UNIVERSITY OF CALIFORNIA PRESS

University of California Press, one of the most distin-
guished university presses in the United States, enriches
lives around the world by advancing scholarship in the
humanities, social sciences, and natural sciences. Its
activities are supported by the UC Press Foundation and
by philanthropic contributions from individuals and
institutions. For more information, visit www.ucpress.edu.

University of California Press
Oakland, California

© 2016 by The Regents of the University of California

Library of Congress Cataloging-in-Publication Data

Shore, Zachary.
    Grad school essentials : a crash course in scholarly
skills / Zachary Shore.
        p.   cm.
    Includes bibliographical references.
    ISBN 978-0-520-28829-4 (cloth : alk. paper)
    ISBN 978-0-520-28830-0 (pbk. : alk. paper)
    ISBN 978-0-520-96326-9 (ebook)
    1. Study skills—Handbooks, manuals, etc.
2. Universities and colleges—Graduate work—
Handbooks, manuals, etc.   3. Graduate students—
Handbooks, manuals, etc.   I. Title.
    LB2395.S545   2016
    378.1'70281—dc23   2015019426

25   24   23   22   21   20   19   18   17   16
10   9   8   7   6   5   4   3   2   1

CONTENTS

Introduction

The Skills You Need

This is a little book with a lot of power. The tips you are about to read, and the skills you are about to learn, are seldom taught. Yet they are essential if you want to save time while boosting your performance.

Anyone working toward a bachelor's, master's, or PhD degree must acquire five key skills: how to read, write, speak, act, and research. Unfortunately, most people never learn to do these things efficiently. That's why too many students read ineffectively, write incoherently, speak haphazardly, act unwisely, and research fruitlessly. If they knew how to streamline their efforts in a sensible, focused, and structured way, they could produce superior work while having more time to relax.

I want to teach you potent methods for mastering these five essential skills, so that you can earn your degree with minimum struggle and maximum success. I want this book to help you get what you want. And I don't just want you to survive in school; I want you to flourish. I want you to perform superbly. I want you to know that you have done your best, and I want your professors and peers to know it, too. All you need are two things: the willingness to work smart and the coach to teach you how. Some of my methods include the following:

For enhancing your writing, I will show you how to:

- Use the Columbo Principle—a technique for keeping you and your readers relentlessly focused on your primary argument.
- Spring-load your sentences—a trick for getting past writers' block, so you'll always know what to write.
- Employ three different formulas for structuring your papers to maximize their clarity.

For giving effective presentations, I will teach you to:

- Apply the HEFTY rules—ways of engaging your audience so you'll never hear a snore.
- Follow a five-step process for overcoming nervousness and speaking with authority.

For efficiently conducting research, I will demonstrate how to:

- Laser in on a topic by compressing your questions into eight words or fewer.
- Impress your professors (and yourself) by condensing your thesis to a single, concrete sentence.
- Bring passion to your projects by linking them to something larger.

These are just a few of the techniques that can boost your performance substantially. I won't just tell you what to do; I will teach you how to do it. I cannot guarantee that all of my methods will work for you. Only a charlatan would promise you that.

I can only tell you that they have worked extremely well for me and for the many students I've taught who learned to employ them. So try them out, adapt them to suit your particular needs, and discard what you cannot use. Once you do, you will discover that much of my advice can save you time and trouble.

This book is aimed at students in the humanities and social sciences. And while grad students absolutely need these methods, any undergraduate who learns and applies these techniques will be at an enormous advantage. But these skills are not valuable only in school. In fact, they are immensely useful in the working world. Most college-educated people will have careers that require them to consume, analyze, and present information. Whether you will be studying corporate reports, reviewing the backgrounds of your clients, grading student papers, or just scanning the news for data relevant to your job, the ability to read efficiently and with purpose will make you more successful. It will not only save you time; it will elevate both your comprehension and analysis of problems. I'm not talking about speed reading. Instead, I'm referring to your ability to gut a text and extract its essence. That skill is the starting point for productivity. Most professions also require you to produce some sort of written work: memos, reports, summaries of meetings, and the like. At some point, most employees will need to present their ideas in front of an audience of their peers and bosses. Strong writing and speaking skills are arguably the two most vital attributes of truly successful people. Fortunately, you don't have to be a gifted public speaker or a natural-born writer to distinguish yourself. You just need to master some very basic techniques of structure and presentation. Once you do, you will greatly increase your chances of success while in school and after you graduate.

Although many types of people can profit from these skills, I wrote this book with a particular kind of person in mind: someone who loves to learn. Some guidebooks about higher education take a cynical view. They portray your time in school as a game in which you mainly need to manipulate the people around you in order to get ahead.[1] This book does not share that view. Instead, I wrote this for people who care about ideas and take knowledge seriously. If you believe that our lives grow genuinely richer the more we understand the world around us, then this book is especially for you. And if you long to make your own intellectual breakthroughs, the tips you will learn here can help bring you closer to that goal. The sad fact is that too many students begin with a noble love of learning, but they end up becoming frustrated, bitter, and jaded. I have seen it happen too many times. Their studies dragged on interminably, and the thing they lacked more than anything else—more than money, time, or desire—was mentorship. Even when their professors were well-meaning and tried to explain the "how tos" of scholarship, they could not explain them in ways that their students understood. I want to change that. I know that each person learns differently, and no single book can reach everyone, but I believe that my methods are accessible to a great many people. I hope you'll be one of them.

So who am I to be writing such a book? I earned my doctorate in modern history at Oxford in three and a half years. I then published four scholarly books in ten years. I did it by a combination of working smart and working hard. Along the way I did postdoc-

1. Consider the popular book by Fredrick Frank and Karl Stein, *Playing the Game: The Streetsmart Guide to Graduate School* (Lincoln, NE: iUniverse, 2004), or the dated but humorous work by Pierre van den Berghe, *Academic Gamesmanship: How to Make a Ph.D. Pay* (New York: Abelard-Schuman, 1970).

toral work at Harvard, spent a fellowship year at Stanford, and have been teaching graduate-level courses to military officers for the past nine years. You can earn a degree at Oxford much faster than in the United States, and my first book was the outgrowth of my dissertation. But even with those qualifiers, I still think it fair to say that I know something about getting things done. I want to share with you some of what I've learned about academic productivity. Too many smart people fail to produce meaningful scholarship at a rate that satisfies them. Years pass, yet no research papers, dissertations, articles, or books are completed. Naturally, productivity should not be the primary goal. Far too much so-called scholarship is generated every year, and most of it will be instantly forgotten. Your aim must be to produce quality scholarship as an undergraduate, in a graduate program, or later, if you continue in academia. I believe that the tips I offer here will help maximize your chances of producing the best work that you can, and producing it within a reasonable timeframe.

CHAPTER OVERVIEW

Each chapter offers targeted, structured approaches to a specific crucial skill. I detail formulas for getting started and tactics for not becoming formulaic.

In chapter 1, on dissecting a text, I explain how to beat the Book Zombies—the evil forces that let you read for hours without absorbing any meaning. I first describe what it means to read for a thesis, using the 1982 comedy film *Airplane II* to illustrate the point. I then offer a five-step method for reading actively in a nonlinear fashion. But I don't just theorize about how this might work. Instead I walk you through the process by analyzing a scholarly text while using this method.

In chapter 2 I explain what it really means to critique a text, and then I show you how to do it. Just as in the previous chapter, I present you with part of a scholarly article and take you through the process of discovering the argument's flaws. The aim is to equip you with an approach that you can apply to critiquing any academic literature.

In chapter 3, "How to Write," I provide three formulas for writing with clarity and concision by employing what I call the Columbo Principle. Each formula shows how to craft the opening of your essay, paper, or thesis. I articulate rules of good writing that will help to avoid what I call the Bartender's Burden. If you don't know what that is, that's great. I've just created narrative tension. I'll teach you how to do that, too.

In chapter 4, "How to Speak," I detail a five-step formula for achieving the two main goals of academic presentation: to engage and enlighten your audience. I also discuss tactics for maximizing a presentation's effect, summarizing them with a mnemonic device for remembering the four key elements of a strong presentation. My main aim in this chapter is to emphasize the value of structure. Clear structure aids clear thinking. And the essence of a strong presentation, just as with good writing, is clarity. Because some undergrads and most grad students will participate in classroom discussions of assigned readings, I also spend time explaining how to manage important and potentially frustrating classroom dynamics, such as big-mouthed peers who try to monopolize the conversation. And I offer tips for overcoming your own reticence and putting your comments forward.

In chapter 5, "How to Act," I discuss how to conduct relationships with professors and peers. Navigating social space is one of the most crucial elements of a successful career, and while it definitely matters for undergrads, it is especially vital in grad school, where your future often depends on the support of your professors. The advice in this chapter is frank and no-nonsense, based on long observation, personal experience, and wide reading on the problems students face in this delicate realm.

Finally, in chapter 6, "How to Research," I describe ways of concentrating your efforts by crafting a project sensibly. I begin by walking you through a five-step technique for finding a research question. The search for a meaningful question is often the most daunting phase, and therefore I illustrate how to generate the right kinds of questions—ones that will both satisfy your own curiosity and benefit your career. The chapter's second half tackles the most common research pitfalls. I will show you how to link your questions to issues of larger significance, foster originality through careful structure, and avoid the most pernicious pitfall of all: drawing conclusions before beginning your research.

So let's get down to it. The first thing I want to show you is how to read at an advanced level. Most people assume that they already know how to read, but in fact they have no clue. They read passively, not actively. They read linearly, not strategically. With the method I'm about to offer, you will soon be working smart—reading less while learning more. But before that can happen, you first need to know what a Book Zombie is, and how to keep it from eating your brain. The answer awaits you in chapter 1.

CHAPTER ONE

How to Read, Part I

Dissecting a Text

Have you ever had the following experience? You are hunched over a book, reading steadily along. The monotone monologue in your head is encountering a stream of sentences. You are turning pages. You are in a trance, when suddenly, as if shocked by an unseen cattle prod, you are jolted out of your semiconscious state to discover, "My God. I have no idea what I've been reading for the past twenty minutes!"

You are not alone. Nearly everyone has been a Book Zombie at some point, probably at many points. This is the result of reading passively, and you must never do it again.

Passive reading is the act of opening a book without direction and attempting to comprehend it by starting at the beginning and reading through to the end. To read with no method, no plan, and no targeted objective makes no sense. We call that "linear" reading, and it cannot help you when you are actually searching for something very specific. It would be like looking for Mr. Zachary Z. Zypster in the New York phone book and saying, "Gee, whiz. This is an awfully big book. I guess I'll start reading from the beginning, at Aaron Archibald Ababa, and keep reading until I find Mr. Zypster. He must be in here somewhere."

I have good news. It turns out that not only do phone books have a way of organizing their information for easy searching, so do scholarly texts. You just need to know how they are structured, so you can find what you need.

I have two goals for this chapter:

1. To save you a great deal of time.
2. To boost both your reading comprehension and retention.

You will achieve these ends by reading actively, not passively. I'm going to offer you a five-step method for active reading. Once you learn it (and this method will admittedly take some time to master), your scholarly performance will dramatically improve—as will your mental health, emotional well-being, and overall shine.

Before we turn to the method, I need to stress some important caveats. This reading method is not appropriate for all texts. It can work extremely well with most scholarly books and articles in the humanities and social sciences, and to a lesser extent with comparable works in the natural sciences. It is not appropriate for canonical works from the premodern and classical periods—the kind we use as original sources, such as Plato's *The Republic,* or Machiavelli's *The Prince.* This is because the method is designed to help you jump around within a text, locate the most salient points, and skim over the less pithy parts. Most modern scholarly writing should lend itself to this process. Less-contemporary and classical writings often are not structured in the same way. They also are probably being assigned so that you will give them a very close read. And that brings me to another crucial caveat.

Read closely and carefully. I am about to teach you how to move in a nonlinear way through a text, but this does not mean that you should not try to read it all. If you have the time, you should certainly read a work in full. That's what I do. But I also use this method first. I jump around inside the text until I have a strong grasp of the author's main point. Only then do I go back and read the text more fully. Naturally, if you don't have time to read the entire work—and often in school you simply won't have the time you really need—this method will at least equip you to find the work's essentials, so that you can follow the discussion in class.

Here is the most basic concept to absorb: you must read for the thesis, not just the content. The thesis is the author's main argument, and everyone has an argument. If you are drinking at a bar and listen to people's conversations, you'll find that where there is debate, there are theses. Picture a conversation between two loutish, drunken sports fans. One extols the virtues of the Yankees; his interlocutor is praising the Red Sox. At root, the Yankees fan is arguing that the pitching staff makes his entire team superior. That's his thesis. And in order to support his thesis our slobbering enthusiast sputters out in slurred speech the statistics of individual pitchers in the starting rotation. Those stats are his evidence. They form the backbone of his thesis. Part of your job as an undergraduate or grad student is to spot the backbone of every thesis, locate its weakest links, and break them.

There are two main reasons why you must read for thesis, not just content. The first is that academia is all about arguments, and students must learn to critique those arguments. Spotting and dissecting an argument (which we call a thesis) is your primary task with any text. You might be assigned five different books on the French Revolution. How many times do you really need to read that a king lost his head? Isn't once enough? You have five different books because each author has a different interpretation of those events. Your first task, therefore, is to identify each author's particular interpretation as expressed in her thesis. Your second task is to take that thesis apart by finding its weakest links. (Starting to get it?) In essence, you are on a search-and-critique mission when you read. You are searching for the thesis, and then you aim to critique it. The "critique" part means that you will be assessing the book's strengths as well as its weaknesses. Your critique must always be balanced. But it helps to begin with a critical eye. No one writes a perfect book, and that's okay. The aim is to advance our understanding. The question is whether any given author has moved us in the right direction. Do her thesis and her evidence stand up under close scrutiny? If they do, then we can consider it a meaningful contribution to the scholarly literature, because it brings us closer to the truth.

Just to be extra clear, since this approach is crucially important to your success, let's try a simple example of active reading. We'll do it by identifying and critiquing the thesis in a brief clip from an old movie. In a scene from the 1982 comedy film *Airplane II*, we see two different news broadcasts. On the American news, the anchorman states that a terrible fire raged through downtown Moscow, leaving death and destruction in its wake. Next we see the Soviet broadcast of the same event, in which the anchorman says something like: "A glorious fire blazed through downtown Moscow, clearing the way for a brand new tractor factory." Although you were probably born long after the Soviet Union collapsed, you might know that Soviet news was highly censored, downplaying or concealing any problems in Soviet society. So let's imagine that we had to critique both interpretations of this event. What would we do? Let's start with the Soviet broadcast.

First, you need to identify the anchor's thesis. The fire was a positive event for Moscow, and perhaps for Soviet society more generally. In contrast, we can say that the American anchor's interpretation was that the fire was a negative event, leaving death and destruction in its wake. Fortunately, both anchors agree on one basic fact: that a fire occurred. The rest is open to interpretation. Just as with the French Revolution, each author provides a different interpretation of the event, whether it's a king losing his head or a fire in the city.

So how would we critique the Soviet anchor's thesis? Start by listing the assumptions he is making.

1. The fire was glorious.
2. It cleared the way for a new tractor factory.

We can question each in turn. The assertion that the fire was glorious is subjective. There is nothing intrinsic to a fire (or almost any event, for that matter) that makes it positive or negative. We typically judge an event's nature based on its effects. In this case it seems that the fire's gloriousness is evidenced by its effect: it cleared the way for a tractor factory. So if the claim about the factory turns out to be suspect, then the fire's gloriousness would also fall into question.

To challenge the second claim, that the fire cleared the way for a tractor factory, you would ask whether there is evidence of preexisting plans for a factory on that location. Had funds been earmarked for such a factory? Are there written records proving that someone of influence previously decided to build such a factory? If not, then the Soviet claim smells fishy to me.

Likewise, if we were to critique the American anchor's claims that the fire was terrible, we would seek evidence of death and destruction. How many people actually died? Can we prove that they died as a result of the fire? Was anything actually destroyed by this fire? Did buildings collapse? You get the point. We are searching for hard evidence to bolster a claim. And if we cannot find it, if the author does not provide it, or if the author's evidence is more assertion than fact, then we can probably break the back of this thesis.

There is a second reason why you must train yourself to read for thesis, not just content. In some undergraduate courses, and in most graduate ones, you will be quickly overwhelmed by the amount of reading. If you try to read every word of every book assigned, you will drown. You will not sleep. You will not eat. Instead, you will become one of the many Book Zombies—gaunt, sullen figures who haunt their department hallways. They appear as apparitions, weighed down by the mass of books loaded in their backpacks, creeping from class to class, unable to articulate a coherent thought. We call this condition "logolapsia" (I just made that up), and it afflicts unsuspecting students who failed to read this slender guide. Sufferers cannot express an author's thesis, because they have not learned to read in an active, targeted manner. Here comes the cure, or the prevention. It is a five-step process with one key technique. I'll give you the overview first, and then I'll explain each step.

HOW TO READ ACTIVELY

Step 1. Analyze the title and subtitle.

Step 2. Scrutinize the table of contents.

Step 3. Read the last section first.

Step 4. Read the introduction.

Step 5. Target the most important chapters of the book, or sections of an article.

Your most useful tactic in this process: restate what you have read in your own words and write it down.

Always remember: restate and write down.

Step 1. Analyze the Title and Subtitle

Titles are clues to the author's thesis. You are on a search-and-critique mission when you read. Your first task is to seek out the author's thesis, and the title and subtitle will often serve as shortcuts. If the title is generic and bland, like *A History of Russia,* then it won't help you much. But if the title is something like *The Clash of Civilizations,* then you have a pretty good idea that the author's main argument has something to do with conflict being along civilizational lines. From that you might deduce that previous works in the field have offered different interpretations of how international conflicts can or will occur: perhaps between states, or within states as civil wars, or along racial, ideological, or class divides. Who knows? The point is that from the main title alone you can begin to extract useful information about the author's thesis. By actually thinking about what the title really means, you are saving time by priming yourself to spot the thesis.

Subtitles, which are the phrases that typically follow a colon, are your next helpful hints. If the full title and subtitle are something like *Group Genius: The Creative Power of Collaboration,* you might guess that the author is arguing against the notion that great ideas arise from solitary brainiacs contemplating gravity under an apple tree. Or consider *Born to Be Good: The Science of a Meaningful Life*. You can expect that the author is making a scientifically based, probably biologically based argument that humans have an inherent tendency to be good, or perhaps merely a capacity to be good. You don't really know, of course, until you read further. You are just priming your brain to be on the lookout for the thesis. What you don't want to do is gloss over the title and subtitle without taking a moment to envision the likely thesis. Defeating the Book Zombies begins by actively thinking about everything you read, starting with the titles.

Step 2. Scrutinize the Table of Contents

Chapter titles are also clues to the author's thesis. Authors are using each chapter to buttress their main thesis. Each chapter serves as a subargument supporting the overall thesis. So take the time to read each chapter title carefully. Go through the same process I just described regarding the book's title and subtitle. Ask yourself what the author might be trying to convey in each chapter. Again, a bland chapter title like "Introduction" or "The Early Years" won't help. But often chapter titles can be highly suggestive of the author's point of view. By the way, subheadings (which are those little titles that separate the sections within a chapter or within an article) can serve the same purpose as all other titles. When you spot them, think about what clues they might be offering.

Consider the book *Triumph Forsaken: The Vietnam War, 1954–1965*. From the title and subtitle you might guess that the author is arguing that America, or someone, could have won the Vietnam War, but someone chose not to win it. When you explore the chapters in the table of contents, you find titles such as the following:

"Insurgency," and "Commitment," and "Attack," but these don't tell you a heck of a lot. Then you spy some other chapter titles, including the following: "Betrayal." Hmmm. I wonder what the author is suggesting. I guess somebody betrayed somebody else. But who could it be? Here's another chapter title: "Self-Imposed Restrictions." Humph. Who the heck would impose restrictions on himself, and why? And another one: "Self-Destruction." So we think back to the main title, *Triumph Forsaken*, and we can surmise that someone had a triumph available to him in this war, yet he defeated himself (or itself, if the culprit is a government or a country). Again, you don't really know anything about this book, and you have yet to read a single sentence. Nonetheless, you have a reasonable sense of where the author might be heading with his thesis. So now it's time to delve into the text and find out.

Step 3. Read the Last Section First

Now that you are primed to locate and identify the author's thesis, go immediately to the last paragraph of the book or article. I do not recommend this method with a mystery novel, but it can be tremendously helpful with scholarly texts. The author typically wants to leave you with her most important idea. If she is thoughtful, in more ways than one, she will encapsulate her main idea in the final paragraph. The thesis is not always there, but it shouldn't be far away. At least it will be in the final section, whether that is a subsection or a concluding chapter. You are searching now for that one golden paragraph, the one that contains the big idea, crisply summarized. When you find that paragraph, *restate it in your own words.*

There is no technique more important than restating the ideas you read in your own words and then writing them down.

The more you do this, the better you will comprehend what you have read, and the more likely you will be to remember it later, namely during class discussions. So get in that habit. *Restate and write down.* And when you do, try using simple words. Don't think that you need to be poetic or highbrow, deftly peppering your synopses with rarified words drawn from your GRE vocabulary list. Forget that. That's not important at this moment. Just crystallize the author's ideas in the simplest terms necessary. Note that I did not say "the simplest terms possible." It is always possible to simplify an idea to the point of making it simplistic, and thereby lose its meaning. You must learn to craft pithy syntheses of others' ideas in the simplest terms necessary— necessary to capture the author's meaning. Naturally you will not do this for every sentence in the text; only for the most important sentences and paragraphs.

Next I recommend reading the first paragraph of the conclusion. If you are dealing with an entire book, this will be the beginning of the chapter entitled "Conclusion," if you are lucky, or simply the final chapter, whatever it is called. If you are dealing with a scholarly article, then there might be a subheading labeled, "Conclusion," or there might be a line break with some white space separating it from the main body of the article, or there might be no clear indication of a concluding section at all. In that event, where no clear concluding section is apparent, you will have to skim backward from the end, looking for key words or phrases that indicate a conclusion. I'll say more about this in a bit.

The first paragraph of a conclusion might contain the thesis, or it might reinforce the thesis that you already gleaned from the final paragraph. Again, you might not find the thesis in either the last paragraph or the first paragraph of the final section, but you are most likely to find it there.

Step 4. Read the Introduction

Now turn back to the introduction and skim it. See how quickly you can come to the same golden paragraph you found in the conclusion. It won't be worded the same way, of course. It is not an exact replica, copied and pasted into the text, but it will contain the same basic concept, expressed in similar language. I want you to use your *restate and write down* technique. Render this golden paragraph in your own words and write it down. Compare it to what you did for the conclusion's golden paragraph. How closely do they match? If they are basically the same, you have probably found the thesis and grasped its essence. That's not a guarantee at this point, but you are probably closer than you think. If your two renderings do not match, then you have either misidentified the thesis and need to read more before you can be certain, or you simply need to modify your understanding of the thesis. There may have been a greater nuance to the thesis when expressed in the conclusion as opposed to the introduction. Focus on the golden paragraph from the conclusion. It is usually the right one.

You might reasonably ask why you did not read the introduction first instead of waiting until step 4. The answer is that introductions often contain the thesis, but conclusions almost always do. Introductions contain all sorts of other information that might bog you down in the beginning of your search-and-critique mission. They might begin with an arresting anecdote. They might review the existing literature and the debates within the field, in the process explaining how their own work contributes to this debate. They might spend pages thanking their friends and family, spouses and mistresses, librarians, archivists, other scholars, and all of the famous people whom they have never actually met, but with whom they wish to be associated. (Usually they spare us by placing this in an acknowledgments section, but sometimes they sneak it into the intro.) Your best bet for quickly locating the thesis will be by scanning the conclusion first. The introduction should help confirm and reinforce your understanding of the thesis, or, as I said, it might cause you to modify your understanding of it.

Step 5. Target the Most Important Chapters or Sections

I hear you asking: how can you possibly know what the most important sections are? Once you know the thesis, it's relatively easy to isolate the key sections. For example, if the thesis is that President Johnson chose war in Vietnam over a chance for peace, then a section on the history of Vietnam's century-old wars with China might be interesting and even useful background information, but it probably won't take you directly to the main evidence supporting the thesis. And it is this main body of evidence that you now seek. Remember, if the Soviet anchorman claimed that the fire cleared the way for a tractor factory, and that this was a good thing, then you must find evidence of plans for such a factory. The author is certain to provide it. But whether her evidence is convincing depends on two things. Pay attention to this next idea. There are only two ways we prove points in scholarship: through empirics and through logic. Empirics are the tangible bits of evidence we can assemble: the severed head of a king, the burned-out building from the fire, the diary of the midwife who tells us how she lived. Logic is the reasoning that rests above the facts. If someone tells you he saw a triangle with four sides, you know he's geometrically challenged. This means that your two lines of attack are to question either the author's empirical evidence or her leaps of logic. As you read, write down the assumptions that the author is making. Later, you will go through your list and ask whether the author supported each claim with adequate evidence and sound logic.

Everything I have just outlined applies just as readily to an article or individual chapter as it does to a book. If you were assigned an article, you would contemplate the title and subtitle for clues to the thesis, scan the subheadings for further hints, and read the last paragraph first. (Obviously, if the last paragraph is a single sentence, you will start with the previous paragraph.) And if you were assigned a chapter from a book, and not the book itself, you would immediately look up the book from which the chapter came. Never—let me repeat this for emphasis—NEVER prepare for a discussion of a chapter without first having considered the entire book. You do not have to read the entire book, but you absolutely must have a general idea of the author's thesis in that book. Why? Because the chapter will serve as one supporting element in the larger argument. And you must always know what the larger argument is. Which brings me to another useful tip.

FIND LINKS TO SOMETHING LARGER

Always link an argument to something larger. Especially when critiquing an article or book chapter, you need to figure out what the bigger issue is. Nearly all scholars are tackling a small piece of a larger puzzle. The analysis of a particular battle likely reflects the author's view of the whole war. Analysis of a particular war might reflect the author's view of how the countries in question have fought other wars, or conducted their foreign policies, or subjugated peoples, or allowed macroeconomic superstructures to shape their actions. Whatever the issue in front of you might be, there is probably a larger puzzle that the author is hoping to solve. You need to know what that bigger picture is in order to understand the article or chapter. So when you finish your search-and-critique mission, after you have identified the thesis and critiqued it, your final step is to link that thesis to the larger puzzle. As you will learn later in this book, this is good training for when you begin your own research, because you, too, will need to link your own narrow research question to a larger puzzle.

ACTIVE SKIMMING

You rarely have time to read every word of every book or article. It's great if you do have the time, but don't bank on it. Given your time constraints, you need to be maximally efficient. Skimming is essential. Once you have decided which chapters to read, scan each chapter to see if there are any subheadings. Use these exactly as you would a title or subtitle. The subheadings are there to give you clues to the thesis and to point you toward the most important bits of evidence. Read every subheading first to gain a sense of the chapter's basic structure. You can then select the most important-sounding subsections to focus on.

When pressed for time, you must skip paragraphs. The paragraph is your author's smallest idea chunk. Sentences are the elements that explain or support the paragraph, but paragraphs are the bite-sized nuggets that allow you to skip around. In general, you should skip in paragraph chunks. Therefore, the indentation is your best friend.

Read each topic sentence—the first sentence of each paragraph—and make a decision: do you read the rest of that paragraph or skip it? Read or skip? That's all you need to decide.

This is a skill that you will definitely improve with practice. So how to make the right decision?

Use your key technique: restate and write down. (You don't need to write anything down if you decide to skip.) Just restate each paragraph's topic sentence in your own words. Remember to use the fewest and simplest words necessary to convey the author's meaning. The topic sentence should express the paragraph's main idea, or at least it should give you a pretty clear indication of what that paragraph is about. Once you grasp the meaning of the topic sentence, you can make a judgment about whether the paragraph is worth your time.

Most scholarly texts have a certain form. The idea in one paragraph will often be supported by numerous subsequent paragraphs. So if you decide that you don't need the information in the paragraph containing one idea, then you can quickly skip all the subsequent paragraphs supporting it. And you can easily determine if the subsequent paragraphs are supporting a previous idea by restating their topic sentences.

PRACTICE ROUND

I'd like to walk you through an article while applying this method. I can't reprint the entire text, as that would violate copyright law, but I can use certain sections of it. When I teach my students how to read in this way, I like to use the historian Marc Trachtenberg's writings, because they are well-structured and clear, though they contain complex ideas.

We're about to skim, or actually just talk about how to skim, an article on the First World War. As I write this book, historians across the globe are intensely focused on World War I because it is exactly one century since the war began. If you know absolutely nothing about World War I, that's perfect. You don't need to know anything. This method is designed to help you get smart fast on any subject in the humanities or social sciences. So let's apply our five-step process, one step at a time.

Step 1. Analyze the Title and Subtitle

"The Coming of the First World War: A Reassessment."[1]

The first thing we do to beat the Book Zombies is to stop and think. Remember that we are on a search-and-critique mission. We are searching for the author's thesis: his main argument. So what might a title like this mean? Clearly it must have something to do with World War I. Because it uses the phrase "The Coming of," it must involve the origins of the war. And when it says "A Reassessment," it must mean that the author is going to reassess something—presumably something about the origins of the First World War. So what exactly could he be reassessing? Most likely he will reassess the reasons why the war came. Let's find out. The purpose of thinking actively about the title and subtitle of any text is that it primes you to be more receptive to spotting the thesis when you meet it.

Step 2. Scrutinize the Table of Contents

In a book's table of contents, each chapter title offers clues to both the argument within that chapter and the type of evidence that will be presented. Within a chapter or an article, the subheadings do the same thing.

1. Marc Trachtenberg, *History and Strategy* (Princeton: Princeton University Press, 1991), ch. 2.

The first subheading in this chapter is: "The Fischer Thesis." Ever heard of the Fischer thesis? No? Terrific. You don't need to. In fact, it's better if you haven't, because that forces you to think about what it could mean. We can guess that some guy named Fischer had a thesis, or argument. And what is that argument likely to be about? Yes! It's probably an argument about the coming of the First World War. And what is the author likely to say about that argument? Will he agree with it or disagree? I hear you guessing "disagree." Of course, we don't know yet what the author will do, but given that his subtitle suggests that he's going to "reassess" something about the coming of the war, you could reasonably guess that he's going to be critical of Mr. Fischer's claims. And of course being critical is what one expects an academic to be. That is, after all, how they earn their living. But in fairness, we don't yet know for sure what the author's view is of Mr. Fischer's thesis. We are simply skimming the subheadings, priming ourselves to spot the author's own thesis when we meet it.

The next subheading is: "The Rigidity of Military Plans." What could this mean? So far we suspect that the author is reassessing, which is to say critiquing, explanations for the coming of World War I. We guessed that the Fischer thesis was one such explanation, or argument, about why the war came. So maybe the idea of rigid military plans was another such explanation. And perhaps the author is going to challenge this idea as well.

The next subheading is: "The 'Cult of the Offensive.'" As it appears in the book, the words "Cult of the Offensive" are in quotes. Let's say that we have no idea what this phrase is about. Since we know we're talking about a war, we can guess that there was some idea at the time about offensive action, and maybe it took on some kind of cult status. Maybe people became wedded to this idea, whatever it was. And perhaps this is yet another explanation for the coming of the war: the adherence to this idea. But who knows at this point? As we continue to read subheadings, we continue to prime ourselves for step 3.

Step 3. Read the Last Section First

Some authors are considerate enough to use the subheading called "Conclusion." If you should find such a marker as this, feel free to do a little jig. The first thing I do is to skim ahead to see how many pages or paragraphs this section contains. I do that merely to get a sense of how much important stuff I'm likely to encounter. If there are only three paragraphs, for example, then I'd better pay extra close attention to every word to be sure I don't miss the thesis. If, on the other hand, the conclusion is eight pages long, then I need to do more active searching. In this case, Trachtenberg was magnanimous, and we easily find a "Conclusion" subheading. If there is no such subheading, look for an empty space between paragraphs close to the end of the chapter. If you don't find that, look for key phrases at the start of paragraphs, such as "In conclusion," "In sum," "To wrap up," "Finally," or words to that effect. As I skim ahead in Trachtenberg's piece, I see that the conclusion is just over four pages long and contains twelve paragraphs.

You will always read conclusions in their entirety, but let's begin with the final paragraph. Before we do, let's remind ourselves what we've established. We have an author reassessing something about the origins of the First World War. We found that he addresses what seem to be different explanations for the war. And we suspect that he is critical of some or all of them. We have surmised all this before ever having read a single sentence.

Now it's time to dissect the conclusion using our most important tactic: restate and write down. We are about to restate in our own words what each sentence says. To do this, use the fewest words necessary to convey the author's meaning. After each sentence, I will give my own restatement in my own words, but you should try doing it yourself before reading my restatement. That way you can compare your version to mine. And don't assume that my version is the better one. As long as you are capturing the essential meaning in a synthesized form, don't worry if your restatement differs greatly from mine. The words you use are not important; it's the meaning that matters.

First sentence of final paragraph:

"During this whole process, this interpretation was accepted because it was what people wanted to believe."

What bad luck! We didn't get a clear, simple thesis statement like we had hoped. This sentence seems to come out of nowhere. We have no idea what the author means by "this whole process," but we can live without that knowledge for the moment. We just want to get a handle on the essential meaning of each sentence, even if our rendering is imperfect at this initial point.

Restated by me:

An interpretation was accepted because people wanted to believe it.

Second sentence of final paragraph:

"It is important, however, that our basic thinking about issues of war and peace not be allowed to rest on what are in the final analysis simply myths about the past."

Restated by me (and try restating it yourself before you read my version):

Our thinking about war and peace should not rest on myths about the past.

Third sentence:

"The conventional wisdom does not have to be accepted on faith alone: claims about the past can always be translated into historically testable propositions."

Restated by me:

Don't just have faith that conventional wisdom is correct. Claims can be tested.

Fourth sentence:

"In this case, when one actually tests these propositions against the empirical evidence, which for the July Crisis is both abundant and accessible, one is struck by how weak most of the arguments turn out to be."

Restated by me:

The arguments are weak.

Note that complex sentences, ones with lots of parts, need to be trimmed down to their bare bones in order to make them more comprehensible. Cut out the parenthetic phrases and clauses and try to locate the sentence's main clause with its subject, verb, and object (S-V-O). In this case, we have S-V-O = "arguments are weak."

Final sentence:

"The most remarkable thing about all these claims that support the conclusion about events moving 'out of control' in 1914 is how little basis in fact they actually have."

Restated by me:

Claims that events moved "out of control" in 1914 are unfounded.

Let's now assemble the restatements because when we combine them, they might give us a briefer, clearer sense of the paragraph's meaning.

People accepted an interpretation because they wanted to believe it. Our thinking about war and peace should not rest on myths about the past. Don't just have faith that conventional wisdom is correct. Claims can be tested. The arguments are weak. Claims that events moved "out of control" in 1914 are unfounded. Remember that we are looking for the author's main thesis. From the final paragraph of the entire text we can see that he is arguing that interpretations about the war are weak. But is that all that the author wants to say? Is he just tearing down the existing interpretations, or is he also offering some interpretation of his own? Perhaps we'll find out as we read further, but this is the type of question you need to ask of any text: what is the author really trying to achieve? To figure this out most efficiently, you must not only synthesize the author's sentences in your own words, you must also question what you are reading. This is what scholars mean when they speak about "engaging" a text. It means to question all aspects of an argument.

I want you to notice one sentence in particular from the restatements above. It's the one that says: our thinking about war and peace should not rest on myths about the past. Note that this sentence is a little different from the others. It refers to a larger issue beyond the article's subject, which is the coming of the First World War. Instead, the sentence references the much broader issue of how we think about war and peace, not just this one specific war. When you encounter sentences that link to a larger issue, pay special attention. The author is usually giving you a hint about his overarching aim.

Now let's turn to the first paragraph of the conclusion. We'll do the same process of restating each sentence in our own words. The purpose is to glean more information about the author's thesis. So far, we are assuming that his thesis is simply that the interpretations for the war's origins are weak and possibly even false.

First sentence of the first paragraph of the conclusion:

"The aim here was not to offer yet another interpretation of the coming of the First World War."

Restated by me:

The article's aim was not to provide a new interpretation for the war's origins. (It looks like we just found the answer to our question above about whether the author was offering his own interpretation of the war's origins.)

Second sentence:

"This was instead meant mainly as an exercise in intellectual housekeeping."

Restated by me:

The aim was to clean up our thinking.

Third sentence:

"There are many claims about the origins of the war that have been accepted more or less uncritically, and the goal here was to test some of the more important ones against the evidence."

Restated by me:

Many claims about the war's origins have been simply accepted. This article's aim was to test those claims.

Fourth sentence:

"What was at stake was not simply our historical understanding of this particular episode."

Restated by me:

More was at stake than just our understanding of World War I.

Final sentence of the paragraph:

"It was really because so much of our thinking today about issues of strategy and foreign policy rests in such large measure on a specific interpretation of the July Crisis that an effort of this sort was worth undertaking."

Restated by me:

Our thinking about strategy and foreign policy rests on our interpreta-
tion of the July Crisis.

And now to assemble the restated sentences:

The article's aim was not to provide a new interpretation for the war's origins. The aim was to clean up our thinking. Many claims about the war's origins have been simply accepted. The aim of this article was to test those claims. More was at stake than just our understanding of World War I. Our thinking about strategy and foreign policy rests on our interpretation of the July Crisis.

What do you glean from all of these sentences? From the conclusion's final paragraph we thought that the thesis was that the interpretations of the war's origins are weak. From the conclusion's first paragraph we can see that the author wanted to test the standard interpretations, and he also tells us why. He says that our thinking about war and peace in general is affected by our understanding of why World War I began. Authors don't always link their work to a larger issue, but they should, and so should you.

The next step in this process is to read the entire conclusion, restating and writing down the main ideas. It will not be necessary to do this for every sentence. For the concluding section, you could limit yourself to restating each topic sentence. Once you are done, it's time to turn back to the introduction. Let's have a look at the first paragraph to see if it reinforces or modifies what we now believe to be the author's thesis and his aim.

Step 4. Read the Introduction

I always scan each section before I read it to get a sense of its girth. The introductory section is roughly two pages and contains five paragraphs. Here's how the article begins.

"The idea that a great war need not be the product of deliberate decision—that it can come because statesmen 'lose control' of events—is one of the most basic and most common notions in contemporary American strategic thought."

Restated by me:

People think that wars can occur by statesmen losing control.

Second sentence:

"A crisis, it is widely assumed, might unleash forces of an essentially military nature that overwhelm the political process and bring on a war that nobody wants."

Restated by me:

People assume that a crisis could cause a war that no one wants.

Third and final sentence of the article's first paragraph:

"Many important conclusions, about the risk of nuclear war and thus about the political meaning of nuclear forces, rest on this fundamental idea."

Restated by me:

Hold on. This sentence should definitely shake you out of your slumber and ward off the Book Zombies. I thought we were reading an article about World War I. I don't know much about history, but I don't think they had nuclear weapons back then. Why is the author suddenly, and in the article's third sentence, talking about nukes?

When you see something jarringly out of place, it might be a clue to the author's larger aim. We don't know exactly what that is yet, but we definitely want to pay attention. So to restate the sentence:

People think the same way about the risk of nuclear war—that it could happen by accident.

Let's try the same process with paragraph two.

"This theory of 'inadvertent war' is in turn rooted, to a quite extraordinary degree, in a specific interpretation of a single historical episode: the coming of the First World War during the July Crisis in 1914."

Restated by me:

The idea that wars can happen by accident, the "inadvertent war theory," stems largely from an interpretation of World War I.

Second sentence of paragraph two:

"It is often taken for granted that the sort of military system that existed in Europe at the time, a system of interlocking mobilizations and of war plans that placed a great emphasis on rapid offensive action, directly led to a conflict that might otherwise have been avoided."

Restated by me:

People assume that offensive war plans caused a war that could have been avoided.

What follows next is a series of quotes. The next several sentences each contain a person's name and a quote about the war. You will often see this kind of structure in the introductory part of a scholarly text. That's because the author is laying out the claims that others have made in order to show that he is not erecting a straw man. He is providing evidence that actual people have made these claims. And presumably the author is going to show how wrong they all are. I'm going to skip over those quotes because our main focus right now is to grasp the author's thesis and his aim.

Let's start employing the method of reading topic sentences (the first sentence of a paragraph), restating it, and then deciding whether to read the full paragraph or skip it. Read or skip: that is the question. Here's how the next paragraph, paragraph 3, begins.

"This basic problem, the argument runs, was compounded by a whole series of other factors."

Restated by me:

There was a problem made worse by other factors.

So we don't know what "this basic problem" is referring to—and that's good. It forces us to read actively. It wakes us up and ensures that we are engaging the text, actually thinking about what's being said as we try to follow a logical flow of ideas. It's at points like these that you have to make a decision. Do you go back and read the previous paragraph in full, or can you continue reading forward even though you're not sure exactly what's going on?

This is the point where my students typically have minor panic attacks. They say things like, "What if I skip something important?" Guess what. You might, especially in the early stages of learning this method. But with practice, you will quickly come to make better decisions about what to read and what to skip. Don't just trust me on this. Try it out for a few weeks. Resist the temptation to read every word in your first encounter with an article, chapter, or book. Obviously, if you have enough time, you should read everything, but rarely will you have that much time. You'll most likely be loaded down with multiple readings from numerous classes, and trying to read every word, as I said before, will deprive you of sleep, hinder your performance, and shatter your spirit. It's worth giving this method a try because it will save you time in the long run, even though you may initially miss some important points in a text.

So let's decide to skip this paragraph about the problem being compounded by many other factors. We can always return to it later if we have time for a second, more thorough pass through the article.

The next paragraph begins:

"The term 'inadvertent war' can have many meanings."

Read or skip? What's your decision? I think this could be important because we know from the opening paragraph of the whole article that the author's thesis involves the idea of inadvertent wars, meaning wars that happen by accident. Maybe here he will define this term that is central to his thesis. We should probably pay attention. In fact, most scholars are concerned with defining their terms. You will discover this repeatedly in scholarly texts. Authors need to define their terms so that readers can be certain precisely what the author is trying to explain. When you meet paragraphs like these, it's wise to pay attention. That said, let's skip it for now because my main purpose is to illustrate this skimming method.

Looking ahead to the next paragraph we find this topic sentence:

"The main purpose of this article is to examine the idea that World War I was in this sense an inadvertent war."

Hallelujah! We have hit the jackpot, my friends. This is the kind of sentence we fantasize about. It is the Rosetta Stone of sentences. (Okay, enough hyperbole. You get the point.) If you ever use a highlighter, use it now. By the way, I recommend highlighting only when truly valuable sentences appear, like this one. Students who don't know what they're doing tend to highlight everything. Resist that urge. Highlights should be shortcuts to an author's main points and key bits of evidence supporting those points. If you highlight too many sentences, you'll be wasting time later when you are reviewing the text.

This sentence is so clear that it hardly needs restating, but let's do it anyway. Try putting it in your own words before looking at how I rendered it.

Restated by me:

Was World War I inadvertent?

That appears to be the main question driving this article. The most important things to identify in any scholarly text are the question, the answer (which is called the thesis), and the evidence on which the thesis is based. Although the author did not pose that wonderful sentence in question form, I think we can render it as a question, because that's what it really means. The author states that his aim is to examine whether the idea that World War I happened by accident is sound. And because we read the conclusion first, we know his answer to this question is "no." His conclusion said that this interpretation was based on myths about the past, accepted on faith, and rested on remarkably little evidence.

So we now have what we believe to be the author's question:

Was World War I inadvertent?

The author's possible thesis:

World War I was not inadvertent.

We have a sense of what his evidence might be: an analysis of the prevailing arguments about this war, such as the Fischer thesis, the idea of rigid military plans, the idea of a cult of the offensive, and so on. However, we would need to read more of the text before we could safely conclude that all of this is correct. And in fact when we do, we find that the author has a more nuanced view. We can discover that greater nuance quickly by reading topic sentences, deciding whether the paragraph is likely to explain the thesis, and if it isn't, skipping it and immediately making the same assessment of the next paragraph. Even though we cannot at this early stage be certain of the question and thesis, we are zeroing in on them much faster than if we had read passively, one sentence after the next, starting at the beginning, without ever restating the key passages in our own words. This method is therefore saving you time and heightening your comprehension.

We have also identified what seems to be the author's larger aim: to assess American strategic thinking about the risks of nuclear war. He claims that this strategic thinking relates to our understanding of World War I.

Although the discussion of this method has taken a bit of time, if you had been applying it to a text without all of my interventions and explanations, it would not have taken much time at all. The actual amount of reading you would have done would have been remarkably little. I would like you to get to the point where you can extract an author's question, thesis, and larger aim within fifteen minutes. And if you only had fifteen minutes to spend on each reading assignment, you could at least go into a class discussion the following day and be able to follow it. With a little bit more time, you can extract the key bits of evidence on which the thesis is based, and then you can begin to critique it by assessing its logic. We'll work on the critiquing skill more intensely in chapter 2.

Condensing Complex Sentences

Sometimes sentences can be overwhelming. They have so many phrases and clauses that our brains have to work overtime just to make sense of them. One way to deal with such troublesome sentences is to chop them down to size. Cut out the chaff and remake them into simple statements by restructuring them. Cut out parenthetical parts and isolate the subject, verb, and object. Here, for example, is the first sentence of the opening paragraph in the first subsection called "The Fischer Thesis."

"In the early 1960s, the German historian Fritz Fischer set off a storm of controversy by arguing that the German government decided to seize the opportunity created by the assassination of the Austrian Archduke Franz Ferdinand on June 28, 1914, and adopted a policy designed to lead to a European war."

Restated by me in simple sentence form:

Fischer argued that Germany intended to go to war after the Archduke's assassination.

I identified the subject, Fritz Fischer, and asked what Mr. Fischer did. He argued. Yes, he set off a controversy, but he did so by arguing. So what did he argue? That Germany adopted a policy. But obviously adopting a policy is not terribly controversial, so that can't be the heart of it. I'm asking myself, as I study this sentence, what's the important issue here, especially in light of what I've already learned about the article so far. I know it's about inadvertent war, so the key phrase would seem to be "designed to lead to a European war." When I condense, I strip out most adjectives, such as European, and I sometimes simplify the wording. That gives me, "Fischer argued that Germany intended to go to war." I might not even need the additional information about the Archduke's assassination, but I'll throw it in there for now since it adds a sense of timing.

The very next sentence of this opening paragraph of the Fischer Thesis subsection reads:

"This thesis was first laid out, rather obliquely, in a chapter in Fischer's *Griff nach der Weltmacht* (Grab for world power) …"

I'm not even going to finish the sentence at this point in my search phase of reading. I can assume that the rest of the paragraph will discuss how Fischer's controversial thesis was presented and perhaps how it was received. I might next read the topic sentences of each subsequent paragraph, condensing and restating them, and decide whether they are worth digging into at this point. I know that the first and last paragraphs of any book, chapter, or subsection are usually the most important, so I'm eager to see what the final paragraph of this subsection says.

"There is no need, however, to resolve the war origins question here. It is sufficient to note that a whole range of interpretations is possible, and that therefore one does not have to take a particularly dark view of German intentions in 1914 in order to question the 'inadvertent war' theory."

Restated in a nutshell:

Let's not worry about the war's origins right now. Germany need not have intended on a war in order for us to question the idea that the war was inadvertent.

And then we look at the very first sentence of the next subsection called, "The Rigidity of Military Plans."

"The argument that the German government consciously and systematically engineered a European war in 1914 is quite weak."

Sometimes there's no need to restate. It's pretty clear. Now we know what the author thinks of the Fischer thesis, or at least an extreme version of it. He thinks it's flawed. We also have a pretty good sense of what this article is about, what its aims are, and how it is structured.

THE RECAP

The reading method I have just described can work with almost any text in the humanities or social sciences, so long as that text makes an argument. The most essential aspects of active reading are as follows:

- Read for thesis, not just content.
- Search for and critique each thesis.
- Use the five-step process to locate and assess the author's question, thesis, and key evidence.
- Identify if possible the author's larger aim.
- Use titles, subtitles, chapter titles, and subheadings as clues to identify the thesis.
- Restate and write down in your own words what each important sentence means.
- Restate topic sentences and skip paragraphs that reiterate or elaborate on ideas you have already grasped.
- Condense complex sentences by isolating the subject, verb, and object.

Book Zombies will eat your brains if you read passively. They'll also wreck your academic experience. Defeat them by engaging a text. Restating key passages in your own words is one of your most powerful weapons against confusion. And as your active reading improves, you'll be able to write and speak with clarity and force. As you proceed through any scholarly text, your five-step process, combined with your tactic of restating and writing down, will do more than just allow you to locate the author's question, thesis, key evidence, and larger aim. It will also ease your way to critiquing the text, which is what we'll focus on next.

CHAPTER TWO

How to Read, Part II

Critiquing a Text

Here's a common student experience. You read one book on a
particular topic, and the author's argument seems very persuasive. You find yourself nodding your head in agreement as you
read. You feel contented, realizing that at last you understand
something that had previously been a puzzle. But your satisfac-
tion is quickly disturbed as you begin the next book on the same
topic. This author has an entirely different, possibly contradictory explanation for the same phenomenon. This new author
seems just as persuasive as the previous one. And then you read
a third book, and the process of confusion continues. Which
author's answer is correct? And how are you supposed to go into
class the next day to discuss these readings if you can't decide
who's right?

Let's take your reading skills to the next level. As you gradually perfect your ability to dissect scholarly texts, you must
also learn how to critique them. Most students find this process
either baffling or torturous. It baffles them because they can't
grasp what they are expected to do. It becomes torturous

if they understand the expectation but have no idea how to achieve it.

So it's time for some straight talk—the kind that no one ever really wants to hear. By the way, my friends call me a "reality-monger." I'm the kind of person who'd rather be told immediately that he has broccoli in his teeth than to go through the whole day only to discover it that night in the bathroom mirror. I know that not everyone agrees, but I think it's far better to suffer the short-term discomfort of conducting a broc-ectomy than to suffer the far greater pain of remembering all the important people you've been repulsing while you smiled at them throughout the day. With that perspective in mind, here's the hard truth about your critiques.

One of the ways that professors assess your intelligence comes from the critiques you make. It's not the only way, and it's not the final way, but it is a major way, and it makes a potent impression. Your critiques reveal how your thoughts work. A powerful critique suggests a logical, analytical mind. It can even indicate your emotional makeup and show sides of your personality. In short, when you offer a written or oral critique, you are flaunting your naked brain. To avoid being arrested for indecent exposure, you will need to know two things—the two main things I want to offer in this chapter. You must fully grasp:

1. What a critique is and is not.
2. The basic method for crafting a powerful critique.

WHAT IS A CRITIQUE?

A critique is an analysis of the author's arguments. It is a rigorous, probing test of the soundness of the author's claims.

Ultimately, either the arguments hold up, or they fall apart, or more likely some of them hold up and some fall apart. Your job is to determine the work's strengths and weaknesses.

WHAT A CRITIQUE IS NOT

A critique is not a book report. Students sometimes think that they are supposed to summarize what the author wrote. A student stands up in class and essentially retells the story of that text. "First the author said this, and then she said that. Later she said this other thing, and then she said something more." This is wrong. Don't do this. That's what you did in middle school. In college and grad school you must *critique* a text. I'll soon explain what that really means.

A critique is also not a complaint. If, in a class discussion about Professor Schnurdelmeyer's pathbreaking piece on nervous breakdowns in late Victorian literature, a student makes any of the following comments, know that these complaints are not critiques:

It was boring.

It was interesting.

The font was too small.

He used Latin phrases, and I don't speak Latin.

He kept saying, "and so forth." That's like totally annoying.

I didn't get it.

I guess he's right.

These are small, unenlightening observations about a text. And by the way, I have heard students make these very comments, and many more just like them, in class discussions. Don't say such things in class. Tell them to your friends when the professor is not around, but don't let your professors or peers think that you don't know what a critique really is.

CHEAP CRITIQUES: DON'T MAKE THEM

You will find it extremely tempting to criticize an author for something she did not do. It will be tempting because it is so easy. If the author wrote about political turmoil in Kenya, you will hear your peers critique the author for not having discussed the turmoil in neighboring Tanzania, or Somalia, or beyond. If the author analyzed mating habits of the three-toed sloth, your peers will charge that this scholar omitted discussion of the two-toed sloth. These are cheap critiques. A book or article, by definition, is a bounded endeavor. Every author must draw limits somewhere, so you can always charge that the author did not explore outside those limits in some way. The only time that such critiques are helpful come when the author's omission dramatically distorts our understanding. For example, suppose you are critiquing a biography of Thomas Edison, and the author failed to discuss Edison's stepmother. (I don't think Edison actually had a stepmother. I'm just making this up for pedagogic purposes.) If it were the case that Edison's stepmother had repeatedly urged Edison to invent a phonograph, and if she had funded his research, then this would be a rather salient omission on the author's part. In other words, if you are going to critique an author for not having done something, that something needs to be essential to our understanding of the subject.

CRITIQUING TACTICS

Before diving into an actual text that we can critique together, I want to give you a big-picture, bird's-eye view of the process. The following are some concepts and methods to keep in mind each time you begin your critique.

Map the Argument

Laying out the argument's basic elements will help you to critique it. Write down the question, the premises, and the conclusion—which is the thesis. List also the key bits of evidence that support it. Use short, simple sentences that accurately convey the meaning. Ask if each assumption can reasonably be made. You can find many books on critical thinking, logical fallacies, and analyzing arguments. There's no need for me to reproduce that material here. For now, here's my synopsis, just to get you thinking in the right direction.

Broadly speaking, you can attack an argument's logic or its empirics. You can attack along three main fronts: the thesis, the methods, and the sources.

Thesis: Ask if the conclusion follows logically from the premises. Could other causes have produced the outcome being studied? Are the conclusions overstated? They often are. Tip: if someone refers to his own work as "pathbreaking," "ground-breaking," or "revolutionary," be suspicious.

Methods: Ask if the methods of investigation are appropriate for the study. Could a different method produce a different and equally plausible interpretation? Are the standards too high or too low; too broad or too narrow?

Sources: Are the sources new or old? If new, do they actually enhance our understanding or merely corroborate what we already knew? If old, are they being viewed in a fresh light that changes our perspective? Are new questions being asked of these old records? Scholarship should advance our understanding of people, processes, or periods. So ask if the text has achieved this end.

If you scrutinize the author's thesis, subjecting it to a rigorous test of its reasoning, you will give a strong critique. If you ultimately conclude that the author is correct, that's fine—though of course it's always more interesting when you can find the flaws in an argument. Remember that no one writes a perfect book or article. There are always weaknesses, but they are often well hidden. If you begin with a challenging mindset, assuming that there are weaknesses to be found, you will probably be rigorous in your critique.

PRACTICE ROUND

Just as we did in the previous chapter, let's tackle an actual scholarly text and critique it. Let's start by using our reading method from chapter 1. Our goal is to quickly establish the author's thesis. Our method tells us that the first step in battling the Book Zombies is to stop and think about titles, subtitles, and all other titles and headings, viewing them as clues to the author's main argument. So let's turn to John Mueller's provocative piece entitled, "The Obsolescence of Major War."

If you guessed that the author's thesis is that major wars are obsolete, I'd say that's a darn good guess. Why can't every author make it that easy? Of course, his argument will most likely be a bit more complex than that, but the title is probably giving us the gist. So what are the first things we need to determine about his argument? We need to know what he means by "obsolete." And for that matter, we also need to know what he means by "major war." What makes some wars major and others minor or middling? It will certainly help if we know how he has defined his terms, but even before we know that, we may still be able to wrestle with the essence of his argument. Are major wars really obsolete? How does he try to prove this? What assumptions does he make in the process?

Notice that we have not read a single word of this article beyond the title, yet we already have a rough idea of the author's thesis and a general sense of what we need to do to critique it. Remember that a critique is a rigorous analysis of an author's argument, its strengths as well as its weaknesses. As we skim through the article, we'll need to keep our goal in mind. We are searching for weak links in the author's chief claim that major wars have become obsolete. But where should we begin our search?

Using our trusty reading method, we'll start with the final paragraph of the piece. Instead of walking you through it, sentence by sentence, it's time to let you tackle an entire paragraph on your own. Don't worry; I'll be right back. For now, I want you to read this carefully and think about the assumptions it contains.

In some respects, then, the fact that war has outlived dueling and slavery is curious. But there are signs that, at least in the developed world, it has begun, like them, to succumb to obsolescence. Like dueling and slavery, war does not appear to be one of life's necessities—it is not an unpleasant fact of existence that is somehow required by human nature or by the grand scheme of things.

One can live without it, quite well in fact. War may be a social affliction, but in important respects it is also a social affectation that can be shrugged off.

Whenever you face an important paragraph, such as one that concludes an entire book or article, try to extract not only the author's thesis, but also the premises on which the thesis is based. Try it first on your own, then look at how I did it. As always, I don't claim that my synthesis is perfect. If you list different points from mine, that's okay. But if we overlap, that's probably a good sign that we're on the right track. If we both pick up on certain points, there's a reasonably strong chance that they are important ones.

Premise 1: war is a social affectation, not a necessity of human nature.

Premise 2: wars are similar to other social practices that are no longer in style.

Conclusion: major war is ceasing because it is like dueling, slavery, and certain other social practices that also fell out of fashion.

Naturally you don't want to read only the last paragraph and leave it at that. You should of course read the entire article using the nonlinear method. You'll jump around the text, scanning it for important-sounding topic sentences. One such important-sounding topic sentence appears just two paragraphs above the final one. It begins by talking about dueling and slavery. Since the author seems to be making a comparison between war on the one hand and dueling and slavery on the other, this paragraph is probably worth taking a closer look at. It's a long one. As you read it, try to synthesize its main ideas by restating each sentence in your own words. Then we'll see if the paragraph causes us to modify our syntheses of the premises or conclusion.

> Dueling and slavery no longer exist as effective institutions and have faded from human experience except as something one reads about in books. Although their reestablishment is not impossible, they show after a century of neglect no signs of revival. Other once-popular, even once-admirable, institutions in the developed world have been, or are being, eliminated because at some point they began to seem repulsive, immoral, and uncivilized: bear-baiting, bareknuckle fighting, freak shows, casual torture, wanton cruelty to animals, the burning of heretics, Jim Crow laws, human sacrifice, family feuding, public and intentionally painful methods of execution, deforming corseting, infanticide, laughing at the insane, executions for minor crimes, eunuchism, flogging, public cigarette smoking.... War is not, of course, the same as dueling or slavery. Like war, dueling is an institution for settling disputes; but it involved only matters of "honor," not ones of physical gain. Like war, slavery was nearly universal and an apparently inevitable part of human existence, but it could be eliminated area by area: a country that abolished slavery did not have to worry about what other countries were doing. A country that would like to abolish war, however, must continue to be concerned about those that have kept it in their repertoire.

The above paragraph provides further evidence of the author's claims. And it supports the premises and conclusions we established after we had read the concluding paragraph. However, there is an additional important idea that the author explained. Did you notice it? It came in the third sentence, when he wrote that other social practices fell out of fashion "because at some point they began to seem repulsive, immoral, and uncivilized." Sentences like these should always catch your attention, because they contain the key word "because." You should be alert to causal claims, and the key word "because" is a useful clue that a causal claim is present. Let's restate that sentence and consider it.

"Other once-popular, even once-admirable, institutions in the developed world have been, or are being, eliminated because at some point they began to seem repulsive, immoral, and uncivilized."

Restated by me:

Some practices ceased, or are in the process of ceasing, because they came to be viewed as repulsive.

We could now modify our synthesis of the author's thesis in the following way:

Conclusion: major war is ceasing because it is becoming viewed as repulsive, just like dueling, slavery, and certain other social practices that also fell out of fashion.

By incorporating the repulsive aspect of the author's argument, we have stated the thesis more precisely.

CHALLENGING THE LOGIC: CRITIQUING IN ACTION

Our task now is twofold. First, we test whether the premises are sound. Second, we ask if the conclusion follows logically from the premises. That's the essence of how you critique a thesis.

Premise 1: war is a social affectation, not a necessity of human nature.

Mueller wrote that war is a social affectation, one that can be shrugged off. I interpreted that to mean that he thinks war is not caused by human nature but instead by socially constructed behaviors. If Mueller is correct that war is a socially constructed behavior and not part of human nature, then he might be correct that war could become obsolete. But if he is wrong—if war is actually a part of human nature—then war cannot become obsolete, unless that aspect of human nature changes. And Mueller does not appear, at least in this final paragraph (which is where he should wrap up his main ideas), to be arguing anything about a change in human nature. It's quite the opposite, in fact. He seems to be arguing that wars are caused by human social practices, and once those practices are considered unfashionable, they fade away.

So the first premise rests on an assumption that war is a social phenomenon, not intrinsic to human nature. Let's turn to the second premise and examine its assumptions as well.

Premise 2: wars are similar to other social practices that are no longer in style.

We can question both aspects of this premise: that wars are similar to other social practices, and that those other practices faded away. Mueller admits that war is not exactly like dueling and slavery, but he nevertheless is making a claim that it is similar enough to suggest that war is becoming unfashionable just like dueling and slavery have become. So is it true? Has slavery faded away? I'd want to know exactly when this article was published. It appeared in 1989, and a few things have happened since then.[1] One of those things is that slavery has spiked. Global

---

1. As I advised earlier, if you are assigned a chapter in a book, you should always look at the book itself in order to glean the author's thesis in that larger work. Similarly, if you are assigned an article, you should always check online to see if the author subsequently published that article as a chapter (or as part of a chapter) in a book. You can then compare the original article with the later version in the book. In this case, Mueller's later version differs subtly from the original article. You will make a strong impression on your professors if you take the time to do this extra bit of research and comparison. You would then point out the ways that the author modified his language in the

trafficking in women and children, who are forced mostly into prostitution and domestic service, has expanded with the increased power of global crime syndicates. Some even estimate that the number of people living in slavery today is greater than at the height of the African slave trade.[2] So it's fair to say that slavery has not faded away at all; it has simply altered its appearance. However, in Mueller's defense we could say that slavery was once socially acceptable. It was seen as perfectly appropriate for presidents of the United States, members of the elite, plantation owners, and other people of means to possess multiple slaves. Today almost no one would view slaveholding as appropriate. That's why the slave trade is illegal and actively hidden from view. So in that sense, Mueller may be onto something.

Now we could go down his list of once acceptable social practices that have allegedly faded away, and we can question each of them to see how they hold up. When we scrutinize each of them, the ledger looks mixed. See what you think. Dueling? Yeah, not too many people settle their disputes with a pistol. Hmmm, on second thought, isn't that what gang members do all the time, just not at twenty paces? And how about bare-knuckle fighting? Maybe Mueller and I hang out at different bars. Okay, I admit I don't hang out at those bars either, but I do talk with people who tell me about the fistfights they get into. I have nothing but anecdotal data, but I suspect the good old-fashioned fistfight is still alive and well, but without concrete data I can't say for sure. Wanton cruelty? The Islamic State's beheadings have occurred more than a quarter-century after Mueller published

---

later published version and ask what those changes suggest about the soundness of his claims.

2. Ethan B. Kapstein, "The New Global Slave Trade," *Foreign Affairs* 85, no. 6 (Nov.–Dec. 2006).

this piece. But he did say he's referring to the developed world, and certainly beheadings are not acceptable. Then how about public cigarette smoking? I think he's got us there. Certainly in the United States it has become viewed as unsavory. So we have to ask ourselves what Mueller is really arguing. Is he saying that these practices faded away altogether, or is he arguing instead that they simply became less common because they became socially frowned upon? Looking back at the text, it seems to be the latter. That is what one of our key sentences suggested:

"Other once-popular, even once-admirable, institutions in the developed world have been, or are being, eliminated because at some point they began to seem repulsive, immoral, and uncivilized."

Some of the practices Mueller listed have ceased, or are ceasing, but that's not true of others in his list. Freak shows, for example, may be even more popular thanks to the internet. It's debatable. We could at least call into question each item in his list. And as we do that, we begin to erode his argument's stability.

Next we must ask if the practices that ceased did so because they were seen as repulsive (or immoral or uncivilized). Again the record seems mixed. Is public smoking ceasing because it's viewed as repulsive or because it's understood to be unhealthy? Perhaps both, but probably it became seen as repulsive because it first became seen as unhealthy. This might be an important distinction. Remember that Mueller appears to be arguing that major wars are ceasing because they, like other once common social practices, are becoming viewed as repulsive. But if the other social practices he cites either did not in fact cease, or if they ceased but for reasons other than their repulsiveness, then Mueller's claim could be shaky. And you are the one shaking it through this process of questioning assumptions.

Now that we have identified one possible weakness in the author's thesis, another becomes apparent. What if war is not sufficiently similar to those other social practices? What if war is distinctive? If you can argue convincingly that war is in fact different enough from those other social practices, then Mueller's claim will not just shake, it will tremble.

Then there's yet another problem. You find flaws in a thesis by uncovering its assumptions. One assumption is that war is sufficiently comparable to other social practices. What's another assumption Mueller is making?

Remember his main claim: major wars, like certain other social practices, are becoming obsolete because they are becoming viewed as repulsive. We've focused so far on the comparison idea. What about the repulsiveness part? What if becoming repulsive does not necessarily cause something to cease? Is it possible that war could be seen as repulsive yet continue nonetheless? Why might that be? Maybe there are other factors at work. Maybe wars are caused by so many factors that even in the face of its ugliness, human beings are still willing to engage in it because it promises certain gains to certain people. What if, to be even more provocative, it is the very repulsiveness of war that attracts some people? If we can construct a persuasive argument that the repulsiveness of war is insufficient to make it obsolete, then Mueller's whole thesis will do more than shake and tremble: it will positively crumble.

Let's review what just happened. First we read and thought about the title as a clue to the author's thesis. We crafted a tentative thesis statement—major wars are obsolete—and then we refined it by reading carefully the final paragraph first. After studying the final paragraph, we stripped it down to its essential premises and conclusion, framing them in short, relatively simple sentences. Next we listed just some of the assumptions on which the premises and conclusion rest. Merely by listing those assumptions on a separate sheet you can identify weaknesses in the argument's logic. Finally, we considered the thesis in parts: first examining the premise that war is like other social practices, and then examining the proposition that repulsiveness could cause war to cease. Through this process we exposed serious possible weaknesses in the author's thesis.

The critiquing process I've just described should be applicable to almost any scholarly text. Following this process you will read the entire article, having primed yourself to zero in on those key sentences that relate to the author's main claims. You will be much quicker to spot important assumptions and dubious logic. In short, you are setting yourself up to make a powerful critique: a rigorous analysis of the author's thesis. And when you stand before your professor and classmates, you won't be afraid of exposing your naked brain. Instead, you will stand strong, confident that your critique is both rigorous and sound.

THE RECAP

- A critique is not a complaint.
- A critique is not a book report: a reiteration of what the author wrote.
- A critique is a rigorous analysis of the author's thesis: its strengths as well as its weaknesses.
- Strong critiques only discuss what the author failed to do *if* that omission is essential to our understanding of the subject.

To make a strong critique, do the following:

- Isolate the thesis in a single clear statement.
- List the main premises and conclusion in simple clear statements.
- Identify the main assumptions on which each premise rests.
- Ask whether the conclusion follows logically from the premises.

These first two chapters on dissecting and critiquing a scholarly text will help you to develop the most basic initial skills you need for success in academia. Don't expect to have read these chapters and have suddenly mastered the methods. As with any skill, the more you practice, the more refined your technique becomes. But sophisticated analysis of texts is merely the first step toward academic acumen. You need strong critical reading skills in order to begin crafting your own written work. You must now focus on producing exam essays, research papers, and eventually master's and doctoral dissertations that demonstrate sensible structure, logical reasoning, and sound conclusions. Fortunately, there are methods that can get you focused on writing and speaking with clarity and verve. The next two chapters will show you how to spruce up your speech and polish your prose.

CHAPTER THREE

How to Write

Most students approach writing as an exercise in abstract modern art. They think that if they just splash a bucket of words across the screen, somehow these words will assemble themselves into a coherent image. Others view their own words as part of a colorful collage, able to be rearranged in whatever order strikes their fancy. Unfortunately, the reader has no idea what is in your head and is ill-equipped to enter it. Your job is to take the reader by the hand and guide her gently through your thought process. You want your readers to know exactly how you got from A to Z: from the question that drives your paper to the answer you discovered. More than this, when your readers arrive at point Z (your answer to the paper's question), they should realize that your answer is the right one. It is your task to help them recognize it. Learning how to do this is one of your most pressing aims in academia.

You have one overarching goal in all your writing: clarity above all else.

Strive for clarity in all realms of academic activity: reading, writing, speaking, and research. The clearer you can think, the clearer you can read, write, speak, and research. And the inverse is equally true. The clearer you can make your reading, writing, speaking, and research, the clearer you will be able to think.

I'm going to do three things in this chapter to help make your writing lucid:

1. Offer tips for getting quickly to the point.
2. Suggest formulas for structuring your papers.
3. Provide tactics for making your sentences sing.

I. GETTING TO THE POINT
Use the Columbo Principle

Long before your time, in the 1970s, there existed a TV character called Detective Columbo, played by the remarkable character actor Peter Falk. One of the most astonishing things about the show was that it enjoyed tremendous popularity despite that the basic plot of every episode was essentially the same. A wealthy person of privilege commits an intricately planned and seemingly untraceable murder, and Detective Columbo, a rumpled, unshaven, working-class cop, solves the crime. More amazing still, the show differed from nearly all other murder mysteries in that we, the viewers, saw the crime committed in the first few minutes. In other words, there was no mystery at all. We knew "who dunnit" from the start. The real mystery was in seeing how Columbo figured it out.

Make your papers like an episode of Columbo. Don't keep your readers guessing what your thesis is. Tell it to us right up front. The mystery (or as we sometimes say, the "narrative tension") comes from our curiosity at how you arrived at your surprising thesis.

2. STRUCTURING FOR CLARITY

Here are three formulas for crafting your papers, each of which employs the Columbo Principle. These methods apply to any form of scholarly writing, from the research paper to the master's thesis to the doctoral dissertation. By definition, these are formulas. If you overuse them, they will make your writing formulaic, which you do not want. So use them to get you started. Once you feel more comfortable with academic writing, you can alter or abandon these methods altogether.

Formula 1: Make Your First Sentence the
Question You Are Trying to Answer

Consider some of these examples:

Why do people tip waiters in restaurants to which they will never return?

How did Tunisia's 2012 revolution affect regional stability?

What are the overall effects of recycling on the environment?

How did Yeats's political views shape his poetry?

Why did Cicero stand for the Senate?

Why are some countries rich while others are poor?

In the sentences that follow, still within the opening paragraph, you will elaborate and explain the question. Your final sentence or two of the opening paragraph will state your thesis.

Let's imagine how one of these opening paragraphs might look.

Why do people tip waiters in restaurants to which they will never return? Tipping is one means of encouraging good service when we dine at that restaurant the next time. But most Americans tip the waitstaff in restaurants on roadside stops, at highway exits, and in places that they are unlikely to visit again. Is this the result of mere habit? Or is it a function of social conditioning? Or do the roots of this behavior reveal something deeper about human kindness? My research suggests that tipping in distant places stems primarily from a deeply ingrained sense of class solidarity.

This paper might go on to argue that Americans tip in distant places because they feel a comradeship with those in working-class jobs. The author might draw on data (and I'm imagining such data; it may or may not exist) showing that wealthier Americans tip less frequently than those in the middle and working classes. What matters here, for our purposes, is not the argument itself, but rather the structure of the opening paragraph. It begins with a question, one that does not have an obvious answer. And if the answer were obvious, you would quickly need to explain that what we assume is incorrect. Next, the subsequent sentences explain the question, making it more specific. It limits the question's scope to Americans, as opposed to all people everywhere. It also explains what you mean by "restaurants to which they will never return." The final sentence then provides an answer to the opening question. This is your thesis: the argument about who dunnit. Thus, within the first paragraph, you have told us exactly what you are investigating and what you have determined. You have just used the Columbo Principle.

The rest of the paper brings forth your data and gradually builds the case for your thesis. This is why we bother to read the rest. We want to know how you got from point A to point Z. Just how did you determine that a sense of class solidarity solves the mystery of distant tipping? Personally, I'd love to know, so you'd better make it convincing. But caution: if you try to scam me, if you try to BS your way to this explanation by omitting counter-evidence, or worse, by fabricating data, you will be caught, and I will be rather sour. When they're hauling you off to academic purgatory, for God's sake don't tell them that you read this book!

Formula 2: *Make Your First Sentence Your Thesis*

An even bolder approach is to hit the reader instantly with your thesis statement. In this formula you do not wait even for the end of the first paragraph. Instead, you make your thesis the very first thing your reader sees. It's as if the murder in the detective show is committed not simply in the opening scene, but literally in the opening shot. From the instant we begin your paper, we will know your bottom line. The rest of that opening paragraph will need to explain the question you are answering and why it matters (the all-important link to something larger). And the rest of your paper will convince us that you are right.

Let's imagine what some of these bold opening sentences might look like.

The effects of "priming" reduce minority test scores.

Tunisia's revolution destabilized Egypt.

Recycling is bad for the environment.

Yeats's republican values made him stress freedom in his poems.

Cicero's hatred of corruption, not merely his ambition, impelled him to stand for the Senate.

Geographic advantages enabled Europeans to dominate the world.

Let's now imagine one of these sentences along with its full opening paragraph. Following the thesis statement, you would provide some context by referring to the question that is driving your paper. You would elaborate on your thesis and link it, even if only fleetingly, to a larger issue.

Geographic advantages enabled Europeans to dominate the world. Scholars from numerous fields have long wondered why some countries are rich while others are poor. Do the disparities in the distribution of global wealth and power stem from racial, cultural, climatic, or other sources? If we understood the roots of global inequities, would we be better equipped to redress them? I maintain that the natural geographic advantages of the Eurasian land mass afforded Europeans an enormous head start in their development. This head start ultimately enabled them to colonize much of the rest of the world. To understand how this complex process unfolded, we must first step back in time to an age before societies existed.

This, in fact, is a rough rendering of Jared Diamond's argument in his bestselling study, *Guns, Germs, and Steel*.[1] Let's consider each sentence above and analyze what function it serves.

Sentence 1 grabs the reader with a bold, declarative statement: *Geographic advantages enabled Europeans to dominate the world.*

Sentence 2 frames the question driving the paper: *Scholars from numerous fields have long wondered why some countries are rich while others are poor.*

---

1. Jared Diamond, *Guns, Germs, and Steel: The Fates of Human Societies* (New York: Norton, 1999).

Sentence 3 elaborates the question:

Do the disparities in the distribution of global wealth and power stem from racial, cultural, climatic, or other sources?

Sentence 4 links the question to an even larger and more important issue:

If we understood the roots of global inequities, would we be better equipped to redress them?

Sentences 5 and 6 further explain the thesis:

I maintain that the natural geographic advantages of the Eurasian land mass afforded Europeans an enormous head start in their development. This head start ultimately enabled them to colonize much of the rest of the world.

If written with care, the final sentences of the paragraph should both arouse the reader's curiosity and transition smoothly to the next paragraph. That is what sentence 7 does:

To understand how this complex process unfolded, we must first step back in time to an age before societies existed.

Beginning your paper with your thesis statement has at least two significant benefits. First, it signals to the reader that you actually have something to say. You are not just flailing around, spilling words on a screen, and talking around an issue without ever getting to the point. This gives the reader (usually your professor) tremendous hope that some concrete ideas will emerge from the paper. Second, it keeps you completely focused as you write. You will continue to ask yourself if what you are writing is supporting your thesis. Naturally, formula 1—putting your question first—achieves this as well, but formula 2—putting your thesis first—does it in a slightly different way. By placing the thesis at the paper's start, you have created a mental shortcut. You can always glance up at the top of your screen and instantly remind yourself what you are arguing. You might think that you are unlikely to forget your main point, but it can happen that you get lost in a tangent as you write. If you ever question whether you should bother including a given paragraph, the opening sentence of your entire paper will help you to decide.

Formula 3: Craft an Arresting Opening

One other way of beginning your papers, though I don't recommend trying it until you have practiced the first two formulas, is to begin with a catchy tale. In this approach you will convey a brief anecdote, typically not to exceed two paragraphs, which both engages the reader and sets up your research question and thesis. I will say more about this method in the chapter on how to speak. For now, let's take a quick look at some arresting openings from two outstanding writers. The point I want to make by giving examples from Hemingway and Orwell is not that you should strive to write like them. That would be setting the bar a bit too stratospheric. Instead, I want only to show you how clever constructions can hook the reader at the outset.

Ernest Hemingway's disturbing short story "The Short Happy Life of Francis Macomber" begins with this sentence: "It was now lunch time and they were all sitting under the double green fly of the dining tent pretending that nothing had happened."

Immediately Hemingway has made us curious. Clearly something had happened, but we don't know what. And why did they feel a need to pretend that nothing had happened? Our minds quickly begin contemplating scenarios and explanations. And now we want to find out the truth.

A few short paragraphs later, Hemingway hits us with another startling sentence. He had been describing Francis Macomber in rather impressive terms. And then we read: "He was thirty-five years old, kept himself very fit, was good at court games, had a number of big-game fishing records, and had just shown himself, very publicly, to be a coward."

Hemingway shakes us to attention through surprise. He set us up to think one thing, and then he startles us by revealing something discordant with our expectations. More than simply surprising us, he also hooks us again. What had Macomber done to reveal his cowardice? We want to find out.

Here's one more example of the hook. In George Orwell's masterful essay "Shooting an Elephant," he begins: "In Moulmein, in lower Burma, I was hated by large numbers of people—the only time in my life that I have been important enough for this to happen to me."

With just one opening sentence, the author manages to switch our brains into active mode. We are impelled to wonder what he could possibly have done to be hated by so many. Was he a murderer, a thief, a scoundrel? And what was he doing in Burma, for that matter? This is the power of a carefully crafted opening. It engages the reader while setting up both questions and answers. Everything that follows should satisfy our curiosity.

Right now I hear you wondering if it's fair to compare the literary techniques of uberfamous authors to the scholarly research papers of students. Do you think I'm trying to give you a complex? Make you feel bad about yourself for not being a Hemingway or an Orwell? After all, isn't academic writing a completely different creature, with its own distinct style and form?

Obviously, academic writing is not identical in form to other types of creative writing. Nonetheless, academic writing actually is creative. You should not be creative with your data, but you can and should be with your prose. The question really is this: does academic prose have to be dull, or can it be engaging? My goal in this book is to help you maximize your abilities. On the one hand, if you have bad ideas, or no ideas, then no degree of clever prose can help. Most professors will see through flowery fluff and wordplay. On the other hand, if you have good ideas, yet weak writing, then your brilliance loses some of its luster. Your good ideas might not be as readily received and appreciated if you present them poorly. But on the third hand, if you have good ideas and you can present them with power, just think what you can do. So take my advice. Invest the time to craft thoughtful paragraphs. One measure that can help is concision, as you're about to see.

3. STYLE TACTICS
Use Orwell's Rules

In 1946, George Orwell published a marvelous essay on politics and the English language, in which he offered six rules for clear writing. They are still just as good today, though they need some explanation. I will list his rules below, followed by my own elaborations.

1. Never use a metaphor, simile, or other figure of speech which you are used to seeing in print.

To put this in my own words: run a cliché check.

I only wish that Microsoft would invent a cliché check just like the spell-check function in Word. Since they have yet to do it, you must make your own. You don't need software; you just need cognizance. If a phrase comes readily to mind, don't use it.

It is probably a cliché. And once you train yourself to be aware of them, you'll start spotting them in every nook and cranny. You will see them multiplying like rabbits, and you'll avoid them like the plague. (See—not so hard, is it?)

2. Never use a long word where a short one will do.

It's the Keep It Simple, Stupid (KISS) principle. Students often think they have to shovel up weighty words in order to sound intelligent, but usually they are simply hiding behind those words. They are inadvertently exposing themselves as posers. Just say what you think. Let the substance of your ideas speak through simple words and short sentences.

3. If it is possible to cut a word out, always cut it out.

This is essentially William Strunk's terse advice as well: "Omit needless words."[2] I call it the "chop shop" rule. Cut out the fat and just keep the meat. Steven Pinker, in his 2014 book on academic writing, *The Sense of Style*, argues that the number of words in a sentence is not what matters. The key, he maintains, is clarity.[3] I agree, to a point. If the reader can follow your thoughts with ease, then a longish sentence is alright. But I am primarily addressing an audience of undergraduates and grad students in this book. And if you are a student, I recommend that you try trimming down your sentences to the fewest words

2. The original version of Strunk's advice for writers was published in 1919. The latest edition is William Strunk Jr. and E. B. White, *The Elements of Style*, 4th ed. (New York: Longman, 2000).

3. Steven Pinker, *The Sense of Style* (New York: Penguin, 2014). Pinker stresses that omitting needless words is sensible, so long as the rule is not taken to the extreme. A sentence must also have style. It should be pleasing to the ear, memorable, and powerful. Not every sentence will be all of these things, but every sentence should at least be clear.

necessary. Bear in mind that you should not use the fewest words possible. Instead, use the fewest words necessary to convey your meaning. As you develop your writing skills, you may wish to craft longer sentences. In the beginning, however, I believe you will be more successful in conveying your ideas if you keep the sentences simple.

Most bad academic writing is turbid. It is muddy, not clear. And this muddiness is typically caused by an excess of words. So if you can possibly streamline your sentences, do so. Let's have some examples of muddy sentences becoming clear by excision. (By the way, whenever you come across a word you don't recognize, take a few extra seconds to look it up.) The following sentences are similar to those I encounter in students' papers every semester.

Muddy: "In this paper it will be argued that an overabundance of stress-inducing factors frequently coalesce to produce diagnosable symptoms of frenetic behavior patterns among those pursuing advanced educational degrees."

See what I mean about lard? This paragraph is positively bloated. The author has slathered on every word he could scoop. We're taking this bad boy to the chop shop. There's too much fat on this bone.

Clear: "Grad students are often anxious."

Muddy: "In this essay it has been asserted that various factors should be assessed when analyzing the merits of British cuisine. In the view of some observers it has been posited that this cuisine may possess certain qualities that make it worthy of serious consideration when selecting a dining establishment."

In addition to being unclear, the above sentences are also vapid. They don't tell us anything. We learn nothing from them. They are just words spilled onto a page with no real value. If you want to write powerfully, you must strip away empty phrases and make a compelling point that is backed up by evidence.

Clear: "British food tastes good. It is nutritious, palatable, and historically proven to sustain a nation. A British restaurant should rank high when choosing a place to eat."

This is a genuinely counterintuitive argument. It takes us by surprise, since few people would argue the merits of British cuisine. The list of qualities in the second sentence (nutritious, palatable, and historically proven) sets up your structure. The reader understands, and will shortly see, that you are going to support your thesis on these three pillars of evidence. With this kind of foundation you don't need to fall back on the hackneyed construction: "This paper will discuss X, and then it will explore Y, and finally it will explain Z." Instead, the clear version of this opening foreshadows what you will do by compressing it into an argument.

4. Never use the passive where you can use the active.

I teach my students this repeatedly, yet their papers come back laden with "In this paper it will be demonstrated that ..." Run a voice check before you submit your work. See if you can demolish passive constructions and rebuild them in the active voice: subject—verb—object.

Examples:

Active voice: I ran the race.

Passive voice: The race was run by me.

Students love passive voice constructions. In fact, I sometimes wonder if they are romantically involved with their passive voice. I have lectured, pleaded, and begged my students not to use passive constructions, and they all seem to understand the difference. And then they turn in papers that are ridden with them. It's as if they're stuck in a bad relationship and can't manage to break up. Or they break up briefly with their passive voice, and then quickly get back together. I think we're dealing with some codependency issues here. The passive voice removes you from the argument. Instead of saying, "I argue that X," the passive voice construction makes you disappear: "It will be argued that X." Many students fall back on their passive voice because they secretly wish to hide behind their words. They're not ready to take ownership of their ideas.

The most popular passive constructions include the following:

In this paper it will be argued that...

The research in this essay demonstrates that...

It will be seen that...

My advice: avoid all similar such constructions. Take the plunge and embrace your individuality. Use the lovable little pronoun "I." And follow it with a strong, active verb.

I argue that...

I show that...

I maintain, I suggest, I assert, I prove...

You do not absolutely have to use the pronoun "I," but whatever you want to do, for God's sake just do it in the active voice. It's okay to use phrases like, "This chapter," or "This paper," but then give us a verb and an object. "This chapter argues that the active voice kicks the passive voice's butt."

Note that Steven Pinker, the cognitive linguist I cited above, challenges the idea of scrapping the passive voice. He correctly observes that passive constructions serve many useful ends. So please also note that I am not advising you to omit all passive constructions—just most of them. You will make your sentences sing, sparkle, and shine more brightly if you favor the active over the passive. Don't eliminate all passive constructions; just try to use them only when it seems sensible to do so.

5. Never use a foreign phrase, a scientific word, or a jargon word if you can think of an everyday English equivalent.

How I wish you could actually apply this rule, but so many fields, such as anthropology, are jargon-laden. Here's an imagined example: "Professor Schnurdelmeyer tends to twist the time of linear matrices in the progress toward oblivion, which both compounds and circumvents the engagement with a multitemporal ontology of the now-space extending into the Anthropocene."

You will likely need to use your field's jargon to some extent until you get tenure. And even after that, if you hope to get published, you'll either have to keep murdering the language, or forge a band of insurgents who will launch their own jargon-free academic journals. But if you can win your professors' approval of jargon-light sentences, you will save yourself much head scratching: your readers' as well as your own.

6. Break any of these rules sooner than say anything outright barbarous.

Orwell in fact breaks his own rule number 4 about the passive voice in the very passage I cited above from "Shooting an Elephant."

"In Moulmein, in lower Burma, I was hated by large numbers of people …" But this works better than "large numbers of people hated me." In this particular case, the passive construction heightens the tension and accentuates that Orwell was the object of that hate. It also reflects a theme in the essay: Orwell's own passive position. Writing is always a judgment call, but in general I recommend the active voice.

7. Get to the bloody point. Please.

I am adding a seventh rule to the list—my own, not Orwell's. But I'd like to think that George would agree, if he had my job. Most student papers waffle on for paragraphs and pages, interminably blathering around the topic without ever getting to the point. I'll call this problem the Bartender's Burden.

To clarify, imagine that you and I go to a bar for drinks. The bartender says to me, "What'll it be?" And I say, "Scotch on the rocks." And then the bartender turns to you and says, "And what'll you have?" And you say (and picture yourself fiddling with your bow tie as you speak):

"Well, my good man, that is a fascinating question. Since the dawn of time, humans have enjoyed various libations. The ancient Greeks were known to ferment sheep's milk inside goat bladders, while the nomadic yak-herding tribes of Outer Mongolia …"

Oh, Lord! Save me, please. This is cruel and inhumane treatment of your professor. Please don't torture your readers with these endless ramblings. I make my students take a pledge, and I'd like you to take it, too. Right now, in fact. Please raise your right hand and state clearly:

"From now on I will get to the bloody point."

One major aim of the formulas and rules I'm offering you is to force you to get to the point immediately. These methods will keep you focused so that you don't flounder about for pages, and they will salvage what is left of your professors' sanity.

The following are some additional tactics that will make your scholarly writing lucid and enjoyable to read.

Use Subheadings

Most scholarly texts contain distinct units of ideas. Typically there is an introduction, followed by some background sections, followed by some sections detailing one's own research, followed by a conclusion. Each unit serves a separate but interrelated function. As you transition from idea unit to idea unit, try creating subheadings. These alert the reader that something new and distinct is about to hit them. Subheadings help both the reader and the author to organize these idea units in their heads. They help us structure our thinking. Rather than splattering paragraphs on the screen, you will be arranging your idea units within carefully delineated boundaries.

Avoid Grandiose Assertions

Since the dawn of time, students have begun sentences with overblown phrases, such as "since the dawn of time." You are setting yourself up for failure if you do. Phrases such as "From time immemorial" or "Everyone knows that ..." immediately raise suspicions. Your readers will be doubting your claims before you even begin to explain them. Another popular one is: "History shows that blah blah." I doubt it. History probably shows just the opposite as well. Make your assertions pointed and well-grounded, or as my old British PhD advisor once told me: "You'll have to make this argument more 'copper-bottomed,'" which led me to think of him as "old Copper Bottom," but don't tell him that. I hope he never reads this. But if he does, I hope he knows how grateful I am that he insisted I back up my assertions. When you use grandiose phrases, you are making such a broad claim that it will be almost impossible to defend. So don't weaken your case with empty offerings.

Don't Tell Us What the Dictionary Says

No paper should contain the sentence: "The dictionary defines X as_____." This is one of the worst, most clichéd formulations. I know you can come up with a more original way of defining your terms or discussing your material. Don't be a lazy writer. What I said about clichés is just as true of sentence structures. If the structure comes readily to mind, you should probably scrap it and invent something fresher. Unless you are writing a paper on lexicography, or the history of encyclopedias, stay away from citing Mr. Webster.

Ensure a Logical Flow

What's wrong with the following sentence?

"Although pistachio is my favorite Häagen-Dazs flavor, the company's financial situation is extremely tenuous."

There is absolutely no logical connection between the two halves of this sentence. Let's try a more historical example. Note that China's Cultural Revolution and the Great Leap Forward are two distinct historical events.

"Throughout the Cultural Revolution Chairman Mao remained intent on rooting out Western intellectuals from Chinese society, yet the Great Leap Forward proved a monumental disaster for the entire nation."

Both halves of the sentence deal with debacles during Mao's leadership, but there is no logical connection between the two ideas.

One of the hardest parts of writing well involves maintaining a constant logical flow.[4] Within each sentence and from one sentence to the next, ideas must follow in a sensible sequence. Too often we become so lost in our own heads that we forget about our readers' minds. Without a consistent logical flow, our readers will be confused. I know only three ways to correct this.

1. Take a heavy dose of Focusin (available only by prescription) and concentrate solely on this issue when you proofread your work.

2. Ask friends to read your drafts, and have them focus on this issue.

3. Read your papers backward, moving one sentence at a time. (This last measure can also help in spotting typos.)

---

4. Some people find that they benefit from a little extra help being logical and organized. The danger in recommending software to aid in this process is that these programs might be overtaken by newer, superior programs by the time this book goes to press. With that in mind, here are some current tech solutions that students and scholars may find helpful.

DEVONthink is an app that helps you organize your files, PDFs, websites, and notes. If you want an extra tool to find your way around your own materials, you might explore this one.

Zotero primarily serves as a citation maker. Like the much older program EndNote, Zotero quickly transforms your book or article citations into the proper format style. It has many added features, including the ability to capture and store webpages, ones which might expire online.

EverNote is a competitor to Zotero with similar features. It boldly promises to "organize your life." Personally, I prefer to organize my own life, but clearly there are those among us who are happy to outsource that chore to technology.

Forge Conclusions with a Twist

Anyone who reads what you write hopes that your thesis will be at least somewhat surprising, because if you tell us what is obvious, then why should we bother to read your paper? Don't be like the nutty scientist who devotes decades of his career trying to prove that light cannot be extracted from earthworm poo. Everyone thought it couldn't be done, and after years of investigation, he proves that everyone was right. Your papers should add value. Even if you end up determining that the conventional wisdom is correct, offer us something insightful on why it is right. Maybe the conventional wisdom is correct but not for the same reasons that everyone believed. Perhaps you can offer us a different way of thinking about the problem. Papers that merely tell us what we already know do not add value, do not advance our understanding, do not get noticed, and should not get you your degree.

Most people simply restate their thesis in the conclusion, and while this helps remind the reader of your argument, you need to do something more. You need to leave the reader convinced that you are right. Here is one way—and it is only one way—to do that.

On a separate screen or page, list in bullet points all of the evidence supporting your argument: the evidence you used throughout the paper. Then rank each piece of evidence in order of its persuasive power. Then lead with your second strongest point—your second-most convincing piece of evidence. Discuss it early in your conclusion.

Next, remind us of your other points. You don't need to reiterate them; you just need to reference them in some fashion. Imagine how the reader will be nodding her head in agreement as she follows your train of logic. By describing how all of this evidence builds your case, you are softening up the reader for the knockout blow. As you expected, you will end with your number one, strongest piece of evidence—the equivalent of the gunpowder-stained glove, smeared with the victim's blood, and embedded with hair follicles that happen to match the accused assailant's DNA. When you close with your strongest point, you leave the reader with good reason to accept your claim.

Later, in the chapter on how to research, I'll stress the fact that scholarship is not, in fact, about rhetoric. It is not, as some mistakenly believe, an exercise in persuasion, in which the one who argues her case best is the one who wins the day. Scholarship is instead a search for truth. Your job is to ask the right questions and discover the right answers. You won't always find them, but at least you hope to bring us closer to the truth by researching and reasoning in good faith. You give it your level best, as the Brits say. It's okay to fail, but it's not okay to argue for the sake of persuading someone that you are right. Pay attention to this important distinction. First you do the research and decide what the answer to your question really is. Once you find that answer, you then lay out your case in the most persuasive manner possible—not to prove yourself right, but to show others the strength of your conclusion. So remember as you write: first you find the answer to your question, and only after that do you present your case in the light of reason.

THE RECAP

Above all else, academic writing must be clear. It seldom is. When it's muddy, I can't help suspecting that the author doesn't know what he's talking about and is hiding behind his words.

Here's a quick rundown of the tools and tips I've offered to get you thinking and writing clearly.

- Use the Columbo Principle. Tell us your question and answer in the first paragraph. That way we'll know (and you'll also know) exactly what you're trying to say.
- Say something surprising. Don't just tell us what everyone already knows. If you must conclude the obvious, tell us something new about an old idea.
- Use any of the three formulas for opening paragraphs.

  Formula 1: question in first sentence.

  Formula 2: thesis in first sentence.

  Formula 3: engaging anecdote in first or second paragraph, followed by question and thesis.

  They might make your writing formulaic, but that's okay in the beginning. As you grow more comfortable and confident, you can branch out into more creative means.
- Use subheadings for structure. These will help you organize your own ideas while also guiding readers through the course of your argument.
- Employ Orwell's rules, but with my caveats. No rule should ever be obeyed mindlessly. Use them only when it is sensible to do so, and you must be the judge.
- Avoid the Bartender's Burden, and get to the bloody point.

Do these simple things, and your ideas will transmit magically from your brain to the reader's mind. And the secret to the magic trick is clarity.

CHAPTER FOUR

How to Speak

You have been asked to give a class presentation on a particular book, article, or other reading—AND YOU ARE FREAKING OUT. You dread looking stupid in front of your peers. You fear your professor will ask you something you can't answer. You feel a crippling panic attack coming on. Or perhaps you are experiencing all of the above and more. Hmmm ... sounds unpleasant. Take a deep breath and know you're not alone. Public speaking is often ranked as the number one, most common fear. Here are some concrete steps that will make it better. I can't completely alleviate your anxiety, and in fact, you should be a little bit nervous. That nervousness can help you to perform well. It puts passion in your voice and energy in your efforts. A little bit of fear is a good thing. It's only when it becomes debilitating that we need to worry. And even then, we can get you through that as well. For now, let's focus on the formulas that will help you maximize your ability.

The advice in this chapter applies not only to classroom discussions and presentations, but also to most forms of scholarly public speaking. If you continue in academia, you will be giving presentations on a regular basis. I know many academics who suffered from horrible pre-presentation anxiety, but eventually they found ways to overcome it. They never came to truly love standing up before a crowd and putting on a show, but they have managed to do what they need to do in order to have successful careers. This chapter is not about the psychological dimensions of public speaking. Instead it is designed to give you structure: a method for approaching your task and a formula for executing the process. If you are feeling anxious, structure can go far to relieving much of your stress. You will have something to hold on to throughout the experience. Oh, and by the way, speaking of holding on, here is one psychological tip. While you are speaking, grip onto something, if no one can see you doing it. If you are standing at a lectern, have something in one hand concealed behind the lectern, like a rubber ball, a beanie bag, or anything that won't hurt you as you squeeze the bejesus out of it. Or keep it in your pocket (if you have a pocket). I sometimes use my steel business card holder. I focus all of the nervousness into that gripping action, then relax my fist, and it actually helps me.

I'm going to do two things in this chapter.

1. Briefly articulate your two main goals in any form of academic presentation.

2. Provide a formula for structuring your presentations.

SPEAKING GOALS: ENGAGE AND ENLIGHTEN

Ultimately, your mission in any presentation consists of just two simple parts. First, you must engage your audience. This means keeping everyone's attention from beginning to end. Not a snore should be heard nor a doodle drawn throughout your time speaking. Second, you must enlighten your listeners. They must learn something from your remarks, even if what they learn is merely your position on an issue and your reasons for it. If you can accomplish only these two things, you will have achieved far more than most speakers.

Most likely your first experience giving a presentation in college or grad school will come when you are asked to critique a particular reading or set of readings. Here is where you can employ the advice in the previous chapters on searching for the thesis and then critiquing it. Soon I'll describe some ways that you can incorporate your critique into your classroom presentation. Before I do, I want to make sure that you realize that those reading skills are just as useful even when you are not presenting. They come in handy every time you have class discussions. Typically someone else will already have started the discussion and explained the author's thesis. If no one has, that's great. It's your opportunity to jump in and summarize what you think the author is really saying. Once the thesis has been established, the discussion will usually move on to assess the strength or weakness of that thesis, or any subarguments contained within the text. Classroom discussions are a vital part of the way you deepen your understanding of ideas. They are also an important way for you to impress your professors. These times are key to developing your academic speaking skills. So let's spend a little time on learning how to manage those situations.

DISCUSSION TACTICS

Before we talk about structuring your presentations, I want to offer some tips on the daily experience of classroom discussions.

Just because you are not giving a formal presentation doesn't mean you can remain silent in class. You will need to participate actively in critiques of each week's readings. The purpose of such discussions should be to gain a deeper understanding of a text. You hope, if the instructor is a skillful discussion leader, that you will leave each class with a clearer, more fine-grained appreciation for what the authors have argued, for the soundness of their claims, and for the larger issues to which those arguments relate. That's a description of a class discussion going well. Unfortunately, discussions sometimes go poorly, but there are tactics you can employ to improve them.

You must participate in class discussions every time your class convenes. I don't want you to hide in class, hoping no one will notice your silence. Probably no one actually would notice your silence, but I want you to feel confident enough to voice your interpretations of each text. The reading tips I offered in chapter 1 should help. However, participation can be especially daunting when overbearing men or women try to dominate the discussion. Beware these obnoxious peers. They populate nearly every classroom. Smarmy, unctuous, brown-nosing types (often with grating vocal tones), they will strive to cut you off at every turn. They will interrupt you when you speak in class, belittle your analysis, and possibly even bad-mouth you to your professors, in subtle, offhand ways, of course. No, you can't shoot them. Better to outsmart them. And if that doesn't work ... form alliances.

It's always better to make friends than enemies, but some people just don't get this simple idea. College and grad school are hard enough: you certainly don't want to suffer through it entirely on your own. And if friendship and camaraderie mean nothing to you, consider the following careerist concerns. Later, if you pursue academia, your peers might be on hiring committees at places you'd like to work. Or they might serve on journal review boards, prize committees, or they might even be reviewing your work. In an ideal world, all such vetting processes would be completely anonymous and fair. And if you find that world, please send me its coordinates immediately. But until such time, it pays to be nice. Nonetheless, some folks just don't get it, and in class discussions they usually have bigger mouths and fewer principles than you.

If you find that certain individuals dominate the discussions every time, and if the professor is a Social Darwinist who likes to sit back and listen, believing that the best students will figure out how to survive, then alliances are your best defense. Band the good people together and take back the discussion. Build each other up in your comments. Hand off the discussion baton to one another. When the obnoxious ones try to interrupt, let them speak for the same amount of time that anyone deserves, but then interrupt them exactly as they did to you. A discussion schema might look something like this.

You: "One of the main flaws in the author's thesis is that he assumes—"

Smarmina, the obnoxious bigmouth, cuts you off in midsentence: "Actually, I don't see where that comment is going. I think that blah blah blah …"

You, following an appropriate interval, just enough to be fair but no longer: "Smarmina makes an interesting point, but I think we really need to focus instead on (insert brilliant observation). Actually, Quan and Janelle and I were speaking earlier and noting that (insert trenchant comments here). Quan, could you elaborate on what you were saying earlier?"

Quan, your kindly and shy friend in class: "Yes, of course. My point was …" And after making his points, he says, "Interestingly, Janelle had an alternative interpretation. Janelle, what were you saying about Schnurdelmeyer's background and how it influenced his analysis?"

Janelle, your supersmart and very polite friend from class: "Well, I was thinking that Professor Schnurdelmeyer's childhood experience of being beaten by his father in a burlap sack probably affected his representation of male authority figures in his work."

And thus you and your friends wrest back some of the discussion time from Smarmina by passing the discussion baton back and forth among you. Obviously, you can't do this all the time, and you absolutely don't want to prevent Smarmina (or anyone else) from having her say, as that would be unfair. You will not put her down or silence her, as she initially did to you and your friends, but you will take charge of your situation in a firm, respectful manner, using your alliances. And I wouldn't be surprised if eventually Smarmina figures out that she can't keep dominating the discussion as she had been. Bullies are often quick to crumble once you stand up to them with greater force. And in this case the force I'm talking about is simple social pressure. She might not want to be the odd person out forever. If she comes around, welcome her in with open arms. It's better to make friends than enemies. One day Smarmina might be serving on those review boards, too.

Here's another common classroom dynamic. Your professor asks a probing question about the reading. You quietly reflect on the question as others state their views. And just when you have formulated your thoughts and feel ready to contribute, somebody else says exactly what you were thinking. And then the discussion moves on to the next question, and you are left feeling like you missed your one big chance to make an insightful point.

One thing that can help is the right vocabulary. Most likely the person who just spoke did not say *exactly* what you were about to say. You probably can add a shade of nuance to the point, and possibly even more. What you need is to jump in. Here are some phrases that can help you feel comfortable doing that.

"I'd like to piggyback on what Bob just said." And then you make the point in your own words, acknowledging that it is similar to Bob's point, but stressing the slight difference.

Other useful words include:

underscore

amplify

modify

highlight

qualify

elaborate on

Do not say "reiterate," because there is no point in repeating the same thing that Bob said. Your aim is to add to the discussion by drawing out greater nuance from our understanding of the text.

Whether in a class discussion, or in making a classroom presentation, or just when reading scholarship for your research, you will be critiquing texts throughout your time in school, and this is true for undergraduates as well as grad students. Undergrads, of course, often have large lecture courses where there is no time for discussion. But even in these large courses you may have separate discussion sections, typically led by graduate students. Those grad students will probably be grading your papers, so don't underestimate the importance of participating in those discussions. Your capacity to critique a text in any discussion will impress your professors, your discussion section leaders, and also your peers. But far more important than this, your active critiquing of scholarship will engage your brain, sharpening your sensitivity to faulty logic. This awareness in turn will make your own academic work stronger.

Now let's take your knowledge of dissecting and critiquing texts and figure out how to let it make you shine on stage.

CRAFTING YOUR PRESENTATION

So if your specific goal with a classroom presentation is to engage and enlighten while critiquing an author's thesis, how do you craft such a presentation? Below I offer a formula to get you started.

Five Iterative Steps

Note the word "iterative" above. It means you will repeat these five steps over and over again until your presentation is ready, or until you run out of time, or until you are so bloody sick of preparing that you would rather confess your love of Justin Bieber on a date with someone you desperately wish to impress than to spend one more second practicing your talk. As always, I'll give you the steps first, and then I'll explain them.

Step 1. Formulate your thesis.

Step 2. Write it all out.

Step 3. Rehearse it alone.

Step 4. Rehearse in front of others.

Step 5. Get feedback and begin again.

You will then repeat the entire process, incorporating your audience's feedback. Let's call this first iteration "Phase Two," and it looks like this:

Step 1. Reformulate your thesis, if necessary.

Step 2. Rewrite the presentation, correcting for errors.

Step 3. Re-rehearse alone.

Step 4. Re-rehearse for others.

Step 5. Receive new feedback (preferably from a different audience) and begin yet again.

Let's go through these steps in turn. In step 1, you decide what you plan to argue. You never get up in front of an audience without an argument. You have a message, a bottom line, a main point you wish to make about what you have read. Make it the same way I suggested in the chapter on how to write, by distilling it down to a single sentence. This punchy, declarative opening can grab your audience's attention and draw them in.

In step 2, you write out your entire presentation. This will help you to figure out what you need to say, and what you need to cut. It will also enable you to time yourself, which is very important. No one likes the presenter who drones on way past her allotted time. If you are asked to speak for ten minutes, do not speak for fifteen or for five. Stick to the time allotted. Too short a presentation looks weak, as though you have nothing to say. Too long a presentation can both bore and annoy your listeners. The only way to keep on time is to rehearse aloud while timing yourself.

In step 3 you speak your presentation aloud in private. You can record yourself if you find that helpful, but the main thing is to feel comfortable saying the words. You should not read from a script. There are few things more boring than listening to someone read from a prepared text. It is far more interesting to listen to someone speak seemingly off-the-cuff. Obviously, you are not speaking off-the-cuff. Instead, you have written out and rehearsed your presentation because you want to ensure that you know what to say. But you do not, and should not, read your text to the class. Of course, many people do this, and many snores are heard among the audience. The exception to this rule is if you are already a master public speaker. Such people know how to memorize their work and present it so smoothly, so effortlessly, and so naturally, that it seems completely extemporaneous. If you can do that, then you probably don't need to read this chapter. If you can't, then take my advice for now. Rehearse your presentation in private, and don't try to memorize every word. Instead, get the general feel for what you want to say and then make notes. It's your notes that you will use in class, not the full text.

Your notes can consist of key words and phrases, the bullet points of your talk. Now is a good time to develop those, right after you have rehearsed aloud in private and trimmed your talk to the proper length of time. Take those notes, plus a valium, and gather together a few good friends. Try to choose honest friends, the kind who would tell you if you have broccoli in your teeth, your fly is unzipped, or your points are incoherent. In step 4 you deliver your talk to them, and ask them to take notes while you speak. At the end, they should be able to tell you what your thesis is, what evidence you used to support it, and, most important of all, exactly how bored they were. Another issue you want feedback on is the precise moments when they were confused. Focus on those. Make sure you restate those points in clearer, simpler terms.

In step 5 you review all of your friends' criticisms, write them out very carefully, study this document thoroughly, and crumple it into a tight little ball. And they call themselves friends? Who the hell are these idiots? Don't they know genius when they hear it? Fire these so-called friends and find new ones— people smart enough to know exactly what you're trying to say without any effort on your part. You need friends who are clairvoyant mind readers. I mean seriously, is that really so much to ask?

The cold, sad truth about speaking and writing is this: no one else has the damnedest clue what is inside your head. Your job in both processes—speaking and writing—is to give others a guided tour of your thoughts. And if you fear being totally exposed, then you're going to have to clean things up in there first. Don't let this tour look like the Minotaur's labyrinth. You want clean, straight lines that lead the listener from A to Z. And since you can't be sure what others are thinking until you ask them, you will have to garner their feedback. Don't be foolish and assume that you can just wing it, refusing to rehearse in front of others before the actual presentation. Practicing before a live audience is the best way to learn just how clear your points really are. Naturally they seem totally obvious to you, because you are in your own head. You can follow the twists and turns of logic, the myriad connections of fragmentary thoughts, the brilliant, staggering epiphanies, or just the mundane musings about when to clip your toenails. But no one else can follow your thoughts as easily. Communicating with clarity is the hard part. The only reliable way I know to achieve it is to inflict your rough practice talks upon your friends and loved ones and hope that their love is true.

Speaking, writing, and for that matter also teaching are not tests of what you know. They are instead tests of how well you can explain what you know to others. Your knowledge of a subject is secondary. It is your ability to communicate your knowledge that matters most. And if others cannot understand what you are trying to say, you failed. (Sorry to be harsh, but you're not paying me to be kind; you're paying for advice that will help.)

The five-step method is one way of structuring your approach to any presentation. Below are some tips on presentation tactics. These are tricks of the trade—additional ways to help accomplish your two main goals: to engage and enlighten.

Four Key Elements

Here's a mnemonic device for remembering the four key elements of a strong presentation. Let's call it the HEFT approach. I'll list the elements and then explain each one in turn.

Hook them at the start.

Enumerate your points.

Flag the transitions.

Conclude with a Twist.

And for those who feel especially relieved when they finish, you can add a **Y** at the end: Yodel for joy that you survived the experience.

HOOK THEM AT THE START

Take the time to craft an opening hook. With good presentations, just as with good writing, the opening frames the audience's experience. If you start out strong, it will be much easier to hold your listeners' attention when you reach the drier parts. Your hook might be a relevant anecdote closely relating to your topic. To be effective, it must be unknown by most people in the class. You certainly don't want to open with a story or quote that is widely familiar. I have seen people do this many times, and it always falls flat. If you're not sure how well-known the anecdote is, test it out on your practice audience and ask around. Alternatively, you could start with a joke, but again, it must not be known by most people in the room, it has to be truly funny (test it out), and above all it must relate to your presentation topic. Those are stringent criteria. If you don't have a joke that fits all three, don't tell it.

ENUMERATE YOUR POINTS

Immediately after your opening hook, or in lieu of it if you choose not to use a hook, try enumerating the points you plan to make. For example, say something like:

> I want to do four things today.
> 1. Summarize the author's main argument.
> 2. Illuminate the key assumptions underlying the thesis.
> 3. Identify the key evidence that the author uses to support her case.
> 4. Critique the thesis by explaining its two principal flaws.

As you speak, you might even raise a finger on one hand for each point you state. This draws your audience's attention to the points and makes it even clearer that your talk has a definite structure. That way the audience knows what is coming, it knows what to listen for, and it helps them to take orderly notes. By the way, I would avoid having more than five parts. Beyond five your talk can seem too cluttered or confusing. Maybe you can pull it off, but you will have to be pretty polished to do it. Some people like to pass around handouts on which the bullet points are listed. This can be an additional visual aid. I never use this technique, but I'm sure it can be done to good effect. Do whatever is most comfortable for you, so long as it helps the listener and you to stay clearly "on message," as they say in politics.

By the way, Steven Pinker, the cognitive linguist I mentioned in the previous chapter, advises against what is called "signposting": the act of listing at the start all the things you are about to do. Signposting in your written work is indeed pretty boring. It deadens the writing at the start. It usually looks like this: "In this paper I will first do X, and then I will do Y. Finally, I will conclude by doing Z." It would be far more powerful to just do it rather than telling us what you plan to do. But speaking is different from writing. It is simply harder for most people to follow your thoughts when they hear them, as opposed to seeing them in print, where they can always scan their eyes back up the page to review what you have written. Audiences need more handholding in order to follow your speech. If you are simply telling a story, then no signposts are necessary. But when delivering a scholarly exposition, you have to remember that most folks are not adept at tracking the main points they hear. As a personal aside, I am blind, and out of necessity I have trained myself over many years to listen with care and identify a speaker's main points. In fact, most of the blind scholars I know have also developed this skill. But many sighted people lack this ability. If you lack it, you can and should cultivate it. And when you are speaking to a group, you need to, as we say in the vernacular, "do them a solid" by making your main points more explicit. Enumerating your points is one way of doing that.[1]

---

1. You might have noticed that I have been signposting at the start of each chapter, outlining what I intend to do. While it is true that signposting typically deadens your writing, this book is an instruction manual. Its purpose is to teach you basic skills efficiently. Therefore, since the aim is different from that of an academic essay or research paper, signposting serves a useful

FLAG THE TRANSITIONS

As you progress through your talk, you should identify the transitions, pausing briefly for your audience to catch up. For example, once you finish your first point or section, you can say, "This brings me to part two," and you name it again, just as you did when you outlined all of the points at the start: "an illumination of the key assumptions underlying the thesis." This wakes the audience up. It snaps them back into focus, just in case anyone drifted and lost the thread of your remarks. It lets them know that you are moving on to the next idea chunk. By pausing for a moment, possibly ten or twenty seconds (which will feel like a long time to you, but is, in fact, not long at all), you are giving your listeners a chance to process what you have said. Remember, as I've stressed before, the audience is not in your head. It is hard to follow someone else's train of thought. You need to hold your listeners' hands and guide them through your thoughts. Clearly enunciated transitions act as signposts saying, "Okay, we're making a slight right turn now, so stick with me."

CONCLUDE WITH A TWIST

Conclusions are always important, so you will want to make a powerful impression. As one writer once observed, good writing involves the administration of timely surprises. Now is the time for a slight surprise. Rather than simply restating everything you have said, which is what most people do in a conclusion, try instead to offer your audience something new. Make a point that

---

purpose. It primes your brain by letting it know what it is about to learn. Signposting also helps your audience when they listen to a presentation, but in contrast, when you write scholarly papers, you should use the methods I've described in the chapter on "How to Write."

goes beyond what you have already said. After synthesizing your own main ideas in the presentation, take us to the next logical inference. Maybe your analysis suggests larger problems with the author's work. Maybe it suggests larger problems with the entire discipline. Maybe your critique hints at areas within the field that demand further exploration. Perhaps your commentary shows how insightful the author truly is, and by comparison how shallow most other works appear. Whatever you conclude, give your listeners something to ponder once you're done. You will then have both engaged and enlightened them. As George Bush said, "Mission accomplished." Hmmm ... on second thought, let's not jump to conclusions. Your final words should invite discussion, not disaster.

USING MULTIMEDIA

I am unashamedly old-fashioned. I barely use any media at all. I was the same way in grad school. No PowerPoint, no flashy videos, no song and dance. I just get up and talk. And whaddaya know? The students actually like it. It's amazing what you can do if you focus on substance.

That said, I realize that many of you young folks—and you know you're getting old when you start using phrases like "you young folks"—have a love affair with PowerPoint. If you truly can't stop yourself, I recommend PowerPoint Anonymous. I hear they have a twelve-step program that can help.

If PowerPoint did not exist, my old-fashioned advice would be to spend your time on thinking through hard problems and devising interesting, original, and clever things to say about your topic. Then just get up there and speak—after you've practiced relentlessly using the five-step process I've just described.

The more you do it, the better you'll get, and the more confident you'll become.

Okay, I admit it. Sometimes, some topics truly benefit from visual representations, especially if you are in a type of social science that relies heavily on charts, graphs, tables, and quantitative data. And sometimes a presentation can also be enhanced by a very short video or audio clip. If this is the case, I urge you to rehearse the use of any multimedia many times before your actual presentation. Too often I have seen students begin their class presentations with an audio clip that no one can hear, a video clip that makes no sense at all, or a PowerPoint slide that is too complicated to follow or too simplistic to impress. If you're going to use multimedia, please show it to your friends during your practice runs, and then test it out beforehand in the classroom before anyone arrives. Ensure that it will go off seamlessly, so you won't be standing in the front of the room, fumbling for several awkward minutes trying to fix a technical glitch.

There is another essential aspect of using multimedia in a presentation. It must relate directly to your talk. Too many students try to play a funny scene from a film, TV series, or YouTube clip, and while it might get a laugh, it has no direct relevance to the topic at hand or the point that the student wants to make. The same standards apply to multimedia as to jokes. They must help you make your main point. If they don't, cut them out.

In short, PowerPoint and similar visual aids can only aid you if you keep them relevant, focused, and smooth. By smooth I mean that you practiced showing them to a mock audience beforehand. Never give a talk without first practicing it in front of a live audience.

THE RECAP

Your primary goals in any form of academic presentation, whether in the classroom or at a conference or in a job talk, are twofold: to engage and enlighten. It is wise to do both, but if you can only accomplish one, please enlighten. Scholars have a reasonably high tolerance for boredom, but they have no tolerance for emptiness. If you are worried that you don't have sufficient ideas to enlighten anyone, take a deep breath, and realize that you are in training. You will learn by doing, and by observing those who do it well. (When you hear a really good presentation, don't just take notes on what the speaker said. Note also how she structured her remarks, how she attacked the central thesis, and anything else that impressed you.) But remember also that you have the techniques from chapter 1 on how to read. That reading method will help you quickly grasp the author's thesis and the evidence on which it is based. And since you followed the most important advice in that method—restating what you read and writing it down in your own words—you will be well positioned to think about the weaknesses of those arguments.

In order to engage and enlighten, practice the five-step iterative method described above. The most important aspect of that method is to gather feedback from your practice audiences.

Additional tips I offered include the following:

- Craft a powerful hook at the start.
- Enumerate the points you plan to make.
- Flag the transitions clearly by stating when you are beginning a new section of the talk: i.e., "This brings me to part two."

· Conclude not only by summarizing your arguments, but also by adding something new, something that links your presentation to a larger issue.

Clear structure aids clear thinking. As your technique improves, you'll be surprised how true this is.

CHAPTER FIVE

How to Act

As you have probably heard, grad school can batter your ego. It's not the place most people should go for warm and fuzzy feel-good sessions. Many Americans find this jarring, because they have been praised throughout their academic studies. Grad students tend to be the higher achievers from their high schools and undergraduate years. Teachers and professors always told them how brilliant they were. And then they arrive at week one of grad school, look around in class, and wonder, "Oh my Lord. What am I doing here? Everyone else is so smart. How can I even open my mouth?"[1]

This is the most common reaction at the start of grad school. I've rarely met a grad student who didn't experience this, except for the truly obnoxious, pompous ones, and the few who

---

1. Although this chapter is specifically directed at grad students, savvy undergraduates can and should profit from the advice I offer. Every undergraduate should know that building relationships with professors is important not just for their grades but also for their careers. As you read this chapter, think how you can apply this information to your situation as an undergrad.

genuinely are brilliant and know it, but there are far fewer of them than you think.

Because so many grad students feel the pressure to seem brilliant, they tend to adopt what they imagine to be an intellectual persona. They become posers. They use jargon too freely, and in general try to act the part of scholar. The condition is so common that psychologists even have a name for it: the "impostor syndrome." It affects not just grad students, but anyone placed in a role that demands knowledge and expertise beyond their ken. In the grad school classroom, it is especially humorous, because every student is imagining that every other student knows more than they themselves do. As a result, each student tries to act even more intellectual, essentially bluffing through discussions in the hope that no one will know how little they know. Two things are tragic about this. First, it leaves the impostor with a gnawing sense that he or she is a fraud, which undermines his or her ability to work confidently. Second, the impostors forget that they are not supposed to be scholars yet. They are scholars in training. Ask yourself this: why the heck would you be in grad school if you already knew what you were doing? Come on, people—you are there to learn. I'm not saying you should act like a fool. I'm just saying that there's no need to pose. If you don't know something, there's always Wikipedia. And if you don't grasp a concept, you should seek out someone who can explain it to you, and keep searching for that someone until you find her. There is no shame in ignorance. There is only shame in staying ignorant because you fear being exposed.

So if you experience moments (or years) of self-doubt, I want to share a secret with you. A lot of your peers are feeling the same way. So chill out, take a few meditative breaths, and accept the fact that if you got into grad school, you can probably get out of grad school with your degree—if you develop the right skills. And while I genuinely recommend meditative breathing, I also suspect that you might appreciate some concrete tips on how to behave. In the preceding chapters I offered tips for developing your grad student skills. These were the mental exercises necessary for getting your analytical brain up to speed. In this chapter I want to focus on your emotional brain. I'm simply going to spell out some real-world advice on the very human side of grad school. Much of this advice involves managing perceptions. Don't underestimate the importance of perceptions. How you act in the presence of your professors can often determine your grades, your funding, and your future. And that, my friends, is the cold, hard truth.

RELATING TO YOUR ADVISOR

What is your advisor's role in your life? Your advisor is the professor who will supervise your graduate studies and the writing of your master's thesis or doctoral dissertation. Before you choose a graduate program, you should contact potential advisors to see if they would be interested in working with you. You should also contact their graduate students to find out what that professor is really like to work with. Because you will be studying closely with your advisor for many years, you will need to build a positive relationship with him or her. If you plan to become an academic yourself, you will want to learn that person's craft, so you will have to create an atmosphere in which your advisor actually wants to train you. And if you do not intend to become an academic, you will still want to build a positive relationship because he or she will help you get through grad school, teach you useful critical-thinking skills, and write your letters of recommendation when you start look-ing for a job.

Many grad students enter their program assuming that their advisor is supposed to be a parental figure: a gentle, nurturing soul, whose selfless energies will be devoted to protecting them from difficulty, fostering their careers, and comforting them when they are blue. Students who believe this might also believe that good always triumphs over evil, that hard work is enough, and that academic success is based solely on merit. Hmmm ... I hate to rouse you from such a blissful dream. So I'll just say, in my most diplomatic manner possible, that it's worth considering some alternative possibilities.

News flash: most advisors, meaning most professors, are pri-marily interested in advancing their own careers. I did not say they are exclusively interested in this; just primarily. I didn't say all of them; I said most. Some of you will be extremely fortunate and wind up with an advisor who actually does devote consider-able time to your well-being. But most of you will be lucky to get timely, useful written comments on your work.

Academics are trained to be scholars first, teachers second. Some are not even very good instructors, despite having taught classes for many years. After being expected to produce first-rate scholarship and deliver excellent classroom instruction, they are next asked to spend their remaining hours on adminis-trative chores for which many are thoroughly unsuited. Profes-sors find themselves caught between the departmental subcom-mittee meeting on chalk purchasing, which just ended at 10 A.M., and the university-wide faculty council subcommittee meeting on the new toilets in Cul-de-Sac Hall, which begins at 10:30. Your professor was hoping to have twenty of the intervening thirty minutes to write a few more lines of his conference paper on the gothic undertones of 1950s Serbo-Croatian cinema when suddenly you appear, as scheduled, to discuss your latest chapter. Your advisor never had a single class, or even a one-hour workshop, on how to be a mentor. He is now being asked to perform a job for which he has had absolutely no training. He may not only lack the patience and temperament for this ill-fitting role, he may also be somewhat deficient in the realm of interpersonal communication skills. Or to put it less diplomatically, he might be a total jackass.

Here's my advice: change your expectations. I didn't say lower them; I said change them. Do not think of your advisor as your friend, your boss, your colleague, your parent, or any other figure. Instead, think of yourself as an apprentice to a tradesman. Your job is to learn a particular craft. Unfortunately, your advisor's job description says nearly nothing about training you.

Imagine you are apprenticed to a master violin maker. Some master craftsmen will patiently demonstrate how the wood is shaped, how the parts are assembled, and so on. Then they will encourage you as you build your own violin, praise the finished product first, and then gently point out its deficiencies and explain how to correct them. Other master craftsmen will simply order the apprentice to build a violin without any explanation of how to do it. After a year, when your creation is at last ready to be inspected, the master takes one glance, finds it unworthy, and smashes it into tiny shards, while simultaneously shattering your heart and soul. Because academic craftsmen possess such wildly varying styles of instruction, you would be wise to learn as much as you can about a potential advisor before choosing one. But because it is not always possible to get the one you want, you might have to deal with a violin smasher. In that event, you must figure out how to extract the maximum amount of instruction possible with the minimum degree of heartache. The first way to accomplish this is by altering your expectation of how you need to learn.

Identify what your advisor does well, and analyze it. Assuming that your advisor is deficient in the mentoring realm, you must become an active learner—someone who does not require step-by-step instructions. (That's what this book is for: just enough hand-holding to get you going in the right direction.) If your advisor has an impressive publication record, study those writings and break them down. Figure out what makes them tick. Take notes on it. Don't just identify the thesis and what it is based on, as I described in the chapter on how to read. Look under the hood to determine how the article developed. And if your advisor enjoys talking about herself and her work, as many academics do, schedule a time to let her discuss herself for as long as she likes. Write down what she says, so that she can see you eagerly transcribing her brilliant tutelage. This will not only help you to learn her craft, it might also make her view you in a more favorable light. Don't do it in a smarmy, ego-stroking way. Do it only if you sincerely want to learn her tricks of the trade.

Perhaps your advisor, despite being interpersonally challenged, is actually a skillful classroom teacher. It does happen sometimes. Don't just attend her classes. Study how she approaches her teaching. How does she structure her lectures? How does she answer student questions? How does she use multimedia? Break it all down and study it as if you had a Stradivarius before you. And if you approach your advisor with a sincere desire to learn this part of her craft, and if you come with specific questions based on studious observations, she might just be impressed by you and thus more generous with her time. In short, you cannot expect your advisor to be a skilled mentor. You will have to take the initiative if you want to learn her craft.

I've just stressed that your learning in grad school is largely up to you. There is a related, equally important point that you must be clear on. Grad students sometimes mistakenly believe that if they don't understand a concept, it's because they're dumb. That's wrong. If the student fails to understand, the fault is with the teacher, not the student. Many professors don't get that basic idea. If you are trying your best to grasp a concept and not getting it, then it is your teacher's job to explain it in a different way, and to keep devising different means until together you find the explanation that makes it clear to you. We all learn in different ways, but many professors have only one method of explaining things. It's easier for them to blame the lack of understanding on the student, not themselves. If they recognized that the fault is their own, then they would need to devote much more time to devising alternative explanations, and time is the one thing that most academics do not possess. So don't blame them: the system is stacked against their becoming good mentors. But don't blame yourself either. If your professor cannot or will not explain a concept to you in the way you need, seek out someone else who can. This might mean contacting other grad students, other professors in your department, or scholars outside your university. Take help wherever you can find it.

DEALING WITH CRITICISM

Throughout grad school, and indeed long after it, you will have your ideas critiqued by your professors and your peers. Don't view it as a personal attack. Separate your sense of self-worth from this process. Know that you are learning a craft, and learning this particular craft requires some mistakes. It also requires learning to defend your ideas without being or seeming defensive. One of the worst things people can do is to appear defensive. That signals weakness, and it usually invites the sharks to draw blood. In other words, they'll rip into you more vigorously if you look vulnerable. Here are some tips for coping with critiques.

Nod sagely when being critiqued; smile when responding.

Listen carefully to what the critiquer is saying. Take notes on it if that helps you organize your thoughts. Jot down key words that get to the heart of the person's comments. All the while that he is speaking, use body language to show that you are focused on the person's remarks, not the person himself. That means you are nodding at the right moments, or making little utterances like, "hmmm," or "ah, yes," and suchlike. When he finishes his remarks, take a moment to collect your thoughts. Silence for a few seconds is fine. Look like you are contemplating what he said. You might close your eyes, or perhaps peer pensively at the ceiling. And then, when ready, smile as you reply.

I usually begin by praising the critiquer for making an insightful comment, if in fact she has. If someone makes a valid point, acknowledge it directly. "You may be right about X," or "You have a strong point about Y." That's the courteous thing to do. And then you must decide on a direction to take. Your options are as follows:

1. Admit that your entire position is untenable, and then collapse into a gelatinous mass of inconsolable tears. (Not recommended.)

2. Admit that the critique is partly correct, but note that those critiques are secondary to the overall point you are making. Critiquers frequently focus on issues peripheral to your main argument. They seek out any weak links in your line of defense and

hammer away at them. Don't let this rattle you. Before you respond, ask yourself if the critique is focused on your central thesis or instead on a minor aspect of it. If the latter, concede the point if the critique is correct, and then refocus the discussion on your main argument.

3. Admit that the critiquer has focused on a central difficulty with your position and thank him for allowing you to discuss the problem more fully, which you might then proceed to do. You would then explain why you believe that your interpretation or assessment is the correct one, but acknowledge that the issue is not clear-cut, which is precisely what makes this such an intriguing problem. This assumes, of course, that your position is not completely undermined by what the critiquer has said. If it is, then you might have to abandon your position altogether. Chalk it up to the learning process. It might happen occasionally, and as the fictional character Omar in *The Wire* would say: "It all in the game."

Receiving criticism is part of the academic process. Don't take it personally. Presumably you are in grad school to learn the craft of an academic discipline. So always be gracious in your responses. When people critique your work, focus on how their comments can make your work better. Regardless of what their actual intentions might be, assume (or imagine) that they are genuinely trying to help you improve. Yes, I know it can be hard sometimes not to feel dispirited, depressed, discouraged, or even personally attacked by other people's criticism. And when that happens, remember that it's your ego talking. It's your ego crying out, "Wait a minute! I just want to be praised. Why aren't you giving me what I want?" The answer is that praise might be what you want, but it's not always what you need. If you truly want to be the best grad student you can be, then override your ego and hear the message beneath the words. The message is always this: your work is flawed and needs to improve. That doesn't mean that you have a flawed character. It's just a comment about a particular piece of work you have produced at a particular moment in time. So figure out what you need to do to improve and get down to business. Time is pressing. The longer you lick the wounds on your bruised ego, the longer it will take to get your degree.

MANAGING IMPRESSIONS

In the first week of grad school, on the first meeting of a class, one grad student announced that he would be tossing a softball around each day before class and invited anyone to join him. It was the first impression he made on his advisor. It was not a serious one. By the way, he never got his PhD. I'm not suggesting that this first impression caused him to fail, but I do believe that he consistently undermined his position by the way he presented himself to his professors. Earlier I argued strongly against posing. I recommended that you not pretend to be someone you are not. Please don't misunderstand what I am now adding to those remarks. My point is not that you should pose as an intellectual. My point is simply that you should conduct yourself like a serious grad student, someone committed to learning—as opposed to someone pretending to know things he doesn't. Here are some sensible ways to demonstrate your seriousness.

Dress appropriately. If you truly are an apprentice to a craftsman, take your apprenticeship seriously, and show it. Dress appropriately for class, taking your cues from both the professor and your peers. Obviously, if your professor wears a tie but none of the students do, you would look like an idiot wearing a tie to class. But on the other hand, dressing in shorts and a T-shirt does not make a professional appearance. So find a happy medium.

Submit work early, never late. Students who repeatedly ask for extensions make a very bad impression. Once in a while is of course understandable, but it should not be the norm. Instead, if you can submit your work ahead of schedule, and if your work is clear and thoughtful (which it is likely to be if you follow the tips in this book), you will look smart and competent. Here's where the organized types have a huge advantage. If you are not an organized person by nature, I recommend forcing yourself to be one while in grad school. If you are a procrastinator, you may want to seek help. Sometimes such people do survive. I have a friend who was printing out his master's thesis just hours before it was due. His girlfriend was at his side, helping him organize the chapters, since he was not printing them in order. The reason for this was that he was actually still writing some of the chapters while printing out others. At one point his girlfriend sweetly suggested that he correct a major error she discovered, and he said, "Well, let's save that for the last minute." At that moment her patience snapped and she shouted, "Honey! This *IS* the last minute!" (By the way, he did eventually get his PhD, but it took more than a decade.)

Keep it positive. If you have never read Dale Carnegie's classic *How to Win Friends and Influence People,* go get it right now and consume it. You would be very foolish not to. It illuminates simple truths about our emotional responses to others, and it offers basic tips on how to manage those reactions.[2]

2. Dale Carnegie, *How to Win Friends and Influence People* (New York: Simon & Schuster, 2009), first published 1936. For an important corrective, you should also read Susan Cain, *Quiet: The Power of Introverts in a World That Can't Stop Talking* (London: Penguin, 2013).

Negativity is a major turnoff in any relationship, be it romantic, professional, or other. Because grad school can beat people down, they tend to reflect their inner troubles back at others. You will spot these students almost immediately. They will invariably be complaining about something, whether it is their financial woes, their incomplete assignments, their lack of progress on the dissertation, or anything else. If you find yourself in such a dark mood where complaining feels cathartic, find a friend or loved one who is not at your university and unload it on him. Do not dump your troubles on your professors. If you have a specific problem that only that professor can solve, then of course you must address it, but do it in as positive a manner as possible. I hope it is obvious that I am not talking about those rare and truly horrible situations, such as a parent's death, a major illness, or some life-altering occurrence. No one is going to feel positive in such circumstances, and you should not pretend to be. Instead, I'm talking about the normal, day-to-day disappointments that can put us in a sour mood. When disappointment strikes, as it does for everyone, try not to show negativity to your professors. If you can keep positive most of the time, you will attract good things to you. It's no great secret; it's just common sense.

Maintain professional boundaries. Because grad students sometimes want to be friends with their professors, they occasionally share too much information. Oversharing about your personal life is, in general, ill-advised. If your professor asks how your weekend was, talk about an interesting book you read. Don't talk about getting drunk, getting high, or engaging in amorous activity. Note my delicate use of euphemism in the previous sentence. Watch your language as well. If you tend to use foul language or crass expressions, save it for your friends and omit it from your interactions with professors. Obviously, if you have known a particular professor for years, and if you have developed a close relationship, then perhaps these rules do not apply. But certainly in the early years while you are getting to know your professors, maintain a professional distance.

Sometimes professors overstep their boundaries as well. Occasionally professors will ask their grad students to perform certain tasks for them, such as housesitting, dog walking, babysitting, restaurant booking, etc. In my view this is inappropriate behavior on the professor's part, although others feel it is perfectly acceptable. The fact is that when it happens it can create an instantly awkward dilemma for the grad student who naturally wants to stay on the professor's good side. Even if you are happy to do these chores, I would not recommend it. It not only blurs the boundary of apprentice to craftsman, it also creates jealousies among other grad students who feel that they are not the professor's favorite, since the professor did not ask them to assist. If a professor makes such a request of you, I suggest politely declining. A dialogue might look like this.

Professor Pushiman: "Oh, Lovelina, would you mind if I had a word with you in my office? I was just wondering if, while I'm away at the conference on representations of masculinity in ancient Roman sculpture, perhaps you wouldn't mind just looking after things at my house."

Lovelina: "Professor Pushiman, I'm flattered that you would think of me and would trust me with your house. Because I have a personal rule of maintaining a strict boundary between student and advisor, I would not be able to do that, but I'd be happy to think if I know anyone who might be available."

Professor Pushiman, slightly recoiling at the intimation that he might have just behaved inappropriately: "Well, it's just some plants that need watering, and a few other minor things. I hardly see how this could be a 'boundary' issue."

Lovelina, smiling broadly but firmly standing her ground: "Oh, Professor Pushiman, it's no problem at all that you asked. And again, I'm truly flattered. Let me think hard about whether I know someone who would feel comfortable doing that for you. And if I find anyone, I'll suggest that they email you directly."

Whatever words you use, the important thing is to make your boundaries clear in a very diplomatic way. Even though the answer will be no, you'll be saying it with a smile. You may be tempted to cave in and simply do the professor's bidding out of fear of offending him. Realize that any awkwardness is momentary. If you remain diplomatic, firm, and pleasant, you will probably earn your professor's respect. He will not see you as a babysitter; he will see you as a bright, tactful, and strong grad student.

FINDING PROTECTORS

It pays to find professors who actually care about you. That's because there may come a time, perhaps multiple times, when you need the good professors to protect you from the bad ones. I'll explain with a story from my own grad school days.

In my first semester of grad school I took a course from a man with a curious personality. Other students, who called him Nutty George, had warned me that he had the unfortunate habit of agreeing to let you write on your choice of research topic, but then insisting that you change the topic completely once you had finished the paper. So, vowing not to let this happen to me, I devised what at the time seemed like a foolproof plan. At the semester's start I wrote up a proposal for a research paper and asked if he would look it over. When we met in his office to discuss it, he said that he thought the topic sounded sensible— at which point I asked if he would be willing to sign my proposal acknowledging his support for the research paper as outlined. He agreed without hesitation. I had him right where I wanted.

And then it was about a week before finals time. Being an organized, type A personality who does not procrastinate, I completed the paper ahead of schedule and handed it to him in his office. He glanced at it and said, "Yes, well ... I think you should actually write on a completely different topic." And then described what he wanted me to do instead. Despite having been warned about this, I was nevertheless stunned by the brazen manner in which he disregarded his earlier commitment. And that was when I made my fatal blunder. "But," I spluttered, "you agreed in writing to my current topic," and fumbled in my backpack for the paper with his signature.

"Yes, yes," he said, waving a hand dismissively. "I know I signed your paper, but I really think that a research topic on blah, blah, blah would be much better."

Now I was stuck. Nutty George had no intention of keeping his word, and I had numerous other papers to write in the closing weeks of the term. So I turned to my favorite professor and told him what had happened. We'll call this man Professor Brutal, only because he liked to tell it like it is: the no-nonsense, brutal truth. When I told him about the signed agreement, Professor Brutal looked for several painful moments at me in silence and then laughed. "Do you mean to tell me that you have been studying diplomatic history all this time, and you still believe that a signed agreement is worth something?"

I felt a sudden rush of shame sweep over me.

Brutal continued, picking up a sheet of paper from his desk and waiving it about, mimicking Neville Chamberlain after signing the Munich Agreement with Hitler. "So you thought you had peace for our time, did you?" And then he did what he always loved doing: abruptly posed a question of me. Occasionally this happened in front of several hundred people in his lectures, when without warning I would have to answer questions on the spot. Fortunately, this time it was just the two of us in his office.

Brutal: "What is a peace treaty?"

Zach: "Uhhh ... what?" I stammered.

Brutal: "What is a peace treaty?" he repeated, this time more forcefully and urgently.

Zach: "Uhhh ... it's an agreement among sides in a conflict to cease hostilities?"

Brutal: "Wrong. A peace treaty is nothing more than a reflection of power relations on the ground. And if one side has the power to break it, it will." He let that sink in, and then continued. "You thought you could get Nutty George to keep his word simply by signing something. But why should he? Do you have the power to hold him to it? What did you plan to do if he didn't keep his word?"

Now I truly felt embarrassed. The possibility that Nutty George, for all his nuttiness, wouldn't keep his word had simply never occurred to me. I had no backup plan at all.

Brutal: "What could you do? Complain to a higher power? Who? The department chair? Do you think he'll care? Do you think the chair even has the ability to make Nutty George, a senior tenured professor, do anything? Will you complain to some union of graduate students? What would happen then? Even if they could somehow hold Nutty George to his word, you'll then have a reputation as a problem-maker, a difficult student, and no professors will want to work with you then."

These were all valid points that I had not considered.

Brutal leaned forward, lowered his voice, and stated: "He has the power in this situation. You don't. And he knows it."

Brutal was right. I had no good options. Protesting could easily make things worse. Nutty George was not a bad man; he was just nutty. If this had been some egregious abuse of power, like a sexual harassment case or something of that magnitude, then any student would certainly have some recourse. But in the scheme of things, his behavior was at worst a major inconvenience and a serious stress. It was not a crime. Too much complaining on my part would probably only have made me look like a whiner, and nobody, and I mean nobody, wants to work with a whiner.

And then Brutal leaned back and provided the solution. "You have a major research paper due for my class. Take an incomplete on that and get it done as soon as you can. But focus now on giving Nutty George what he wants, and don't ever take a class with him again if you can help it." I grinned uncontrollably, and I'm sure Professor Brutal was grinning on the inside. I think he may have even added, "Now get out of here."

Brutal's lessons were many, but the most important ones for your purposes are as follows. Soberly assess the power relations as dispassionately as you can. Avoid unstable professors if possible. Cultivate protectors. And never assume that people will keep their word. Fortunately, they often will. But sometimes they will screw you. When they do, ask yourself if it is really because the person is a bad guy, or do his actions stem from something else? This is a crucial question in any conflict. What is the source of the other's actions? Rarely is the person acting out of evil—

a psychopathic desire to make you suffer. Usually it's something far more mundane, like arrogance, obtuseness, or fear. In this case, Nutty George was probably just used to getting his way, and no one had been able to stop him. Maybe, if enough students had banded together and formally complained to the department chair, they might have been able to effect a change. And sometimes that's the right thing to do. But is it worth your energy? People like Nutty George probably figure that the rest of us don't have the energy to devote to countering their bad behavior, and they're right. We all have to pick our battles, and in my view, this one wasn't worth fighting over. I reasoned that it was wiser to scrap the research paper I had put months of work into, chalk it up as a tough lesson learned, and give him what he wanted. Others might reasonably have chosen to fight it. The problem is that there will always be battles to come, and you don't want to deplete your energy, spend your reputational capital, or get sidetracked from your studies by engaging in relatively minor conflicts. It is better to save your energy and good name for those fights that truly matter. If a professor or peer harasses you, plagiarizes you, steals your work, or harms you in any meaningful way, that's the time to take more serious action. Most likely, those times will be very rare, if they happen at all. But just in case you encounter a problematic professor, it helps to have some protectors. Cultivate relationships with those good professors by reading their work, talking with them about it, and showing that you are serious about scholarship—and a pleasant person as well.

BEHAVIOR IN THE ARCHIVES

[Note: The following section offers advice for how to act when working in the archives. If you have no need of archives, skip this section. I will also have a section on working in the archives in the next chapter on how to research.]

Several fields of study beyond history require archival research. Increasingly political scientists are seeking facts to support their theoretical claims. Scholars of literature often plumb the private papers of noted authors. At times anthropologists, sociologists, behavioral economists, or anyone investigating human behavior, may find it necessary, even profitable, to delve into the detritus of other people's written remains. If you should find yourself in such a predicament, embrace it. But there are a few things you should know.

Increasingly scholars can tap online repositories for records once accessible only in print. Naturally, your first search will always be online, and your professors should be able to point you toward the best online collections. I don't want to focus here on how to conduct research in the digital realm, since there are books devoted to this subject. I do want, however, to say one thing about Wikipedia: it's a fine place to start but not to stop. Wikipedia is not, in my classes at least, an acceptable source. I think it's a great way to get the basic facts about a subject, as long as you never forget that some of those facts could easily be wrong. Scholarship should be rigorously vetted before it is published. Sometimes the vetting process fails, but at least the process has a good chance to remove an author's errors and strengthen her claims. In other words, you can rely on the accuracy of scholarship much more than you can on Wikipedia. So again, let Wikipedia help you get familiar with a subject, and then dig deeper into the scholarly literature.

If the records you need are not accessible online, you will have to do it the old-fashioned way by traveling to an actual archive somewhere far from home.

What do you think is the most important quality you need when working in the archives? Brains? Tenacity? Patience? Immunity to dust mites? All are important and indeed necessary. But what you really need in addition is charm.

Charm will help get you what you seek. After that, you'll need the brains to make sense of it. But good people skills can unlock the gates to crucial records, because every gate has a gatekeeper. Your task is to befriend the archivists who are guarding the most precious papers. But before I explain why, let's understand how to approach the papers that are already accessible.

Every archive has lists of its holdings, some of them available online. You will page through these catalogues, ticking off the collections of documents that seem most likely to be fruitful. Initially the number of records will seem overwhelming. The only way to be efficient is to know your questions before you walk through the door. In the next chapter I will describe how to craft a research question in just eight words or fewer. Using this method, let your question drive your source selection, not the other way around. If instead you allow the sources to determine your questions, you will be lost. There is, of course, one important exception to this rule. You might discover something in your sources that spins you off in a different direction from the one you initially envisioned. That's okay. Use your gut to follow any leads that seem valuable. Often a good research project can emerge from such unexpected finds. You begin with certain questions in mind, but in the process of reading records you might discover related questions and a trail leading to their answers. Follow that trail, if you think it can truly offer meaningful information.

Often, however, the best records are not listed in the standard catalogues. No, my friends, they are hidden from us, and only

the archivists know about them. Or they are listed in the catalogues, but when you request them, they are mysteriously una-
vailable. Here is where your social skills can pay enormous divi-
dends. Chat up the archivists. Get to know them. You can learn
much from their experiences, and if you genuinely find people
interesting, this should be fun. However, if you are in the
humanities yet you do not like humans, or if you are in the social
sciences yet feel antisocial, then this will prove more challenging. Nonetheless, I strongly suggest you overcome your reluc-
tance and brush up your small talk. Because if you can form a
connection with an archivist, he or she might just get you access
to some true gems.

When I was doing my doctoral research in Germany, I always
made time to get to know the people working in each archive.
One time, after a thirty-minute conversation, I started to make
my way out of an archivist's office. Just as I was at the threshold,
thanking her for her time, she said, "Oh, by the way, Herr Shore."
I turned back to her. "There is one set of documents that might
interest you."

"Yes, go on," I said smiling.

"Well, we haven't had the time to list them in the catalogues
quite yet." It turned out that she was offering me seldom-seen
NKVD records (forerunner to the KGB), which the Germans
had purchased just after the Soviet Union's collapse. Those documents wound up being extremely useful in my dissertation.

This type of scenario is not at all uncommon. One of my old
advisors told his students how he was working in a French archive
where the archivists were notoriously stingy with the records
they were willing to share. Realize that if the archivists don't want
you to see something, they can easily make it impossible for you
to gain access. In this instance my advisor happened to catch one

of the head honchos leaving the archive at closing time, so he offered to take the man for a beer. A few hours later, and quite a few beers more, they were laughing and swapping stories. The next day a wealth of new records suddenly came my advisor's way.

The point here is delightfully simple: make friends with archivists, and you might just discover a gem. If you are neutral, you will get what everyone else gets. And if you foolishly make enemies by being demanding or complaining, you can probably kiss that archive goodbye. That treasure trove will never be mined by you.

THE RECAP

- Treat the relationship with your advisor as one between apprentice and craftsman.
- Don't be a poser. If you don't understand something, seek out the explanation.
- Accept criticism with equanimity.
- Maintain professional boundaries with professors.
- Stay positive whenever sensible to be so.
- Cultivate relationships with possible protectors—the professors who will help you in times of need.

How you act determines how you are perceived. And how you are perceived will profoundly influence your success, whether you realize it or not. It is tempting to imagine that academic success is based entirely on merit. There are those rare scholars whose brilliance is so remarkable that their social skills don't matter. If you are such a person, you can perhaps ignore the advice in this chapter, but before you do, just think how much more successful you could be if you combine your brilliance with some social sense. The fact is that everyone can profit from old-fashioned people skills. Don't forget that scholars are people, too. The social skills I've been describing are in some respects no different from the reading, writing, speaking, and research skills. All are techniques without which you might survive, but with which you can truly flourish.

CHAPTER SIX

How to Research

How you think determines how you read, write, speak, and research. And how you read, write, speak, and research reflects how you think. Clear thinking yields clear outcomes. If right now you are biting your nails or reaching for a sedative to settle your nerves because you fear that your thinking is muddled, fear not. The great news is that you can train yourself to think more clearly by implementing the methods I've been outlining. All of the formulas, structures, and tips I've been suggesting throughout this book are not just practical tools for working efficiently, they are also mental exercises that will bulk up your analytical brain. That's why in the introduction I called these methods "working smart." It's not just a smart way of working; it's also a way of working that helps make you smarter. And you're going to need all the smarts you can muster, because you're about to take on the Godzilla of scholarly skills. You are about to shift from consuming knowledge to producing it, and in the early stages it ain't gonna be pretty.

There is no one right way to do research, but there definitely are some wrong ways. In this chapter I want to do three things:

1. Explain your research goal.
2. Provide a five-step process for finding a research question.
3. Offer research tactics to make your research focused, efficient, and meaningful.

Too many students never receive proper guidance on how to conduct research, despite that most will take courses on research methods. The advice below should fill in some of the gaps, save you a great deal of time, and make your final product much stronger. Note that although there are some elements of research that are applicable to all disciplines, every field, and even most subfields, have particular research methodologies, so you'll need to consult books and advisors for specific advice on your field's approach.

But first, it's time for some painful straight talk for those seeking doctoral degrees. I need to say something that you might not want to hear. But you need to hear it, and hear it calmly, without jumping to conclusions. Here it comes.

Because it is extremely hard to make an original contribution, not everyone can write a doctoral dissertation. It is not enough simply to put your mind to it, if your mind does not work in that way. This doesn't mean you're dumb. It just means it's not the right thing for you to spend your time doing. Only you (with advice from your advisors) can determine whether you have the ability to make an original contribution. Often advisors get this wrong. They misassess their students. They assume that the student cannot write a dissertation, when actually the student just needs a clearer explanation of how to proceed. I am convinced that many people who drop out ABD (All But Dissertation) could, in fact, have completed an original work. They just didn't have proper tutelage. No one ever sat down with them and explained how to go about it. That is the purpose of this book: to help you maximize the likelihood of getting the degree you seek.

So how do you do it? How do you even approach the writing of an undergraduate research paper, a master's thesis, or a PhD dissertation? I'm going to gear my comments toward PhD students, but my advice applies to any student seeking to improve his or her performance.

Let's start with baby steps, because if you get off on the wrong foot, you'll be crawling around aimlessly, stacking up incompletes. If you are a master's or PhD student, you'll be whimpering ten years later that your dissertation is nearly complete. Tens or hundreds of thousands of dollars in debt, in your thirties or forties with no experience on your resume, you'll be lamenting to your friends that your parents just don't understand. "Dissertations take time," you'll tell them. "It's harder than you think." And the tragic part of this pitiful tale is that you'll be right. Dissertations do take time, and they are surely harder than most people realize. But these sad facts won't matter when you're teetering on the brink of personal bankruptcy or feeling soul-crushed each time another friend buys a new house, gets a fat Wall Street bonus, or jets off to Jamaica for vacation, while you're stuck in Peawinkle Hall, scratching out a lesson plan for your minimum wage teaching assistant's job that your department handed you out of pity, a responsibility to take care of its own students, and a poorly masked note of glee at the chance to exploit cheap, desperate labor thanks to the iron law of wages. (You can't shake the feeling that as you left your department chair's office you heard her making a faint "ka-ching" sound.) Many such people eventually drop out, swelling the statistics of the ABDs—those who finished All But the Dissertation.

In order not to be a statistic and instead earn your degree, you must first know your overarching goal.

I. RESEARCH GOAL: ANSWER A MEANINGFUL QUESTION

Put simply, your goal is to answer a meaningful question. That sounds straightforward enough, but you would be surprised by two things. First, many people don't grasp that the question must be meaningful. It must lead to an answer that advances our knowledge of something that genuinely matters. (I'll say more on this point later.) Second, many people have difficulty distinguishing among three things: a research topic, a research question, and a research answer, which we call the thesis.

The topic is the general area you are investigating. Maybe it's early nineteenth-century Peruvian labor movements, or representations of madness in the works of Shakespeare, or the social skills of North American academics. These are topics, and too many students mistakenly think that a topic is what they are writing about. It isn't. You are writing about a question and searching for its answer.

The question is what drives your research. It is what gets you up in the morning, keeps you plugging away all day, and it wrangles you out of bed in the middle of the night to jot down an idea for how to solve it. The research question is what you are actually writing about. It could be something like these:

Why were early nineteenth-century Peruvian labor movements effective?

How do nations effectively combat corruption?

Why are some fashion trends long-lasting?

Why were most of Shakespeare's crazy characters women? (I
have no idea if there were more crazy women or men in
his plays. I'm just demonstrating how you might craft a
question.)

Why are most scholars socially awkward?

The answer is your thesis. "Answer" and "thesis," in this
case, are synonymous. Your dissertation is the proof of your
thesis.

When you attend a departmental mixer, or when you are
making chitchat at any cocktail party, and someone asks you
what you are working on, you need to be able to punch out three
short sentences. You need to be able to say: my topic is X; my
question is Y; and my answer (or thesis) is Z. Boom, boom, boom.
No hesitation, no hemming and hawing. Just clear, crisp, polished statements. (This quick synopsis of your work is often
called the "elevator pitch.") This will not only impress your professors, it will give you an enormous boost of confidence. These
three sentences will also be extremely helpful on the job market, regardless of whether you are interviewing for academic or
nonacademic jobs. Obviously, you will not be able to describe
your thesis until you have reached the latter phase of your dissertation. You must never, never draw your conclusions before
you have done the research. (I'll soon say more about this issue,
too.) In the early and middle stages of the dissertation, you
should be able to articulate your topic and your question. Here
are some real examples, as opposed to the ones I invented above.

Here is how I synthesized my own dissertation research at cocktail parties, and on the job market.

My topic was foreign policy decision making in prewar Nazi Germany.

My question was: how did Hitler make decisions?

My thesis was this: Hitler's power to make informed decisions was limited by the very system he created.

Each of these sentences invites the questioner to probe deeper—assuming he hasn't already drifted into a peaceful slumber while you were speaking. Actually, this method of short, punchy statements, one sentence per element (topic, question, thesis), can be an effective means of generating genuine interest in your work. Many students, not to mention scholars, have the unfortunate tendency to drone on at great length—which in today's micro-attention-span, tweet-ridden society means to speak for longer than twelve seconds. Instead, if you can keep parceling out tiny packets of information about your work, you allow your interlocutor to process what you have said and determine if she wants to know more. In that way, you will be able to gauge her interest level while simultaneously demonstrating your clarity of mind, articulate nature, and impeccable social skills. Try it. But practice it with friends before trotting it out at the next departmental mixer.

One of the surest signs that a student doesn't know what he's doing comes when he is asked what his research is about. That's when the undirected student launches into a protracted explication of early American brass rubbings and their vital significance to the national heritage—without ever articulating a research question. This happens because the student either does not yet have a clear question, or worse, he does not understand that he is not simply meant to write about something. This student thinks that his work is meant to tell a story about some subject. That is why he cannot get beyond the vague explication of a topic. No one explained to him that a research project is meant to answer a meaningful question. And in order to answer a question, you must actually have a question to begin with.

Finding the right question is often the hardest part of the process. In a moment I'll offer a method for finding your question, but first I want to make two key points. You must care about your question, and you must understand what a research question is meant to do.

Whenever you are given the freedom to choose your own question, you should find one that you genuinely yearn to answer. (Yes, I really do mean yearn.) You need to be truly curious about this question, because that curiosity will drive your research. It will help you to bring passion to the page, which will make the process much more fun. It will also engage your readers, since they will sense your passion through your words. Don't ignore this touchy-feely-sounding advice. It is more important than you realize. If you are not honestly seized by a question, then the research can become a chore—a protracted, painful chore. Like a Sisyphean torture, you'll be pushing your research boulder up the mountain all day long, only to watch it tumble back down each night. Curiosity is what transforms that experience into fun. When I started in the archives my first time, I worried that the process might be boring. But because I genuinely yearned to know the answers to my questions, the act of sifting through papers for more than a year felt like a suspenseful quest. And that, my friends, is how geeks are made.

Obviously, curiosity is not enough. In addition, your question must fill a gap in the literature. It must tell us something we don't already know, as well as something that we actually need to know. When you first have an inkling about a possible research question, you must see if anyone else has answered it. Most likely someone (or several someones) already has. Don't be discouraged. If no one has answered it, find out why. Is it because it cannot be answered, or because no one recognized its significance? If it has been answered, ask if the answers are complete or satisfactory. Often scholars can only tackle one small piece of a larger puzzle. That's an opening for you. Maybe the existing answers are incomplete: they cover certain aspects of the problem but not others. Alternatively, often the answers given are unsatisfactory: they just don't add up or make sense to you. If you find the existing answers confusing, that's a good sign. It might mean that you are just confused and need someone to explain it to you. But it might also mean that the existing answers are bunk: shallow platitudes that don't stand the test of logical reasoning or empirical evidence. When that happens, you're in luck. You may have just found your question.

But let's assume that you're lost. You have to write either a research paper, a master's thesis, or a doctoral dissertation, and you've no idea what to write about. Either nothing sounds sufficiently interesting, or too many things sound interesting. Here's some advice on how to find your question. As always, I will list the steps, and then I'll explain each step in turn.

2. FIVE-STEP QUESTION-FINDING PROCESS

1. Ask the experts.
2. Get the two most recent books on your subject.
3. Get the next ten most recent books on your subject.
4. Ask if they make sense.
5. Ask the experts again.

1. Ask the Experts

The best place to start in your search for a question is to talk with the people who know the literature best, who should be your professors. Think of them as living literature reviews. They should be able to rattle off some of the outstanding questions in your field. At the very least, they should be able to point you toward the most important recent works, in which you can find a discussion of such questions. If your professor hands you a question, you're in luck. If not, and in fact even if she does, you should still go through the following steps.

2. Get the Two Most Recent Books on Your Subject

Take those two books and gut them in the same way I described in "How to Read." Extract and write down their questions and the answers they give. Are the questions the same, or close enough to each other that we can consider them as essentially the same? If not, how are their answers different from each other? Write it down in no more than a paragraph. Are you sufficiently intrigued by the subject that you would want to continue reading other books about it? If not, then drop this subject and start again with the two most recent important books on another subject. Keep doing this until you find a subject of sufficient interest to you that you genuinely want to keep reading on it. This should be a subject with questions that seem like puzzles to you: challenging puzzles with no easy solutions.

Once you find a topic that really gets you hooked, comb the bibliographies of those two books for ten more related titles and progress to step 3.

3. Get the Next Ten Most Recent Books on Your Subject

Do exactly the same thing with these ten books that you did with the first two. Write down their questions and answers.

4. Ask If They Make Sense

Think about what I described above. Are the answers complete? Have the authors missed a piece of the puzzle? Probably they have. For example, in a sociological study of urban crime, maybe the literature offers explanations ranging from poverty to culture to prejudice. But maybe no one has yet explored the ineluctable pressures of the justice system. Maybe scholars have not adequately examined how police requirements to arrest rather than counsel, or judges' requirements to sentence rather than warn, have conspired to create a system that is rigged to produce more crime, not less.[1] That notion will only occur to you by reading widely on a subject, understanding the standard questions and their explanations, and being dissatisfied with them. If you are dissatisfied with the conventional wisdom, you are probably hot on the trail of your question. When you think you have it, condense it to eight words or fewer. (I'll explain this process in a moment.) Then turn to step 5.

5. Ask the Experts Again

With your possible question in hand, go back to the experts to make sure you are on the right track. Your professors can tell you

---

1. This is a rough rendering of the sociologist Alice Goffman's work on urban crime. See Alice Goffman, *On the Run: Fugitive Life in an American City* (Chicago: University of Chicago Press, 2014).

if your question has already been answered. If so, verify that your professor is right. Don't take his word for it. In academia we question everyone and everything. Often the best research results when someone refuses to accept the standard explanations. Your professor will refer you to the book or article where this question was definitively settled. Dissect it as you have learned to do. Decide for yourself if that answer is satisfactory and complete. If not, you might be getting very close. You'll just have to convince your advisor that the standard interpretations are flawed and that your question is worthy of further research. (And if you can't, you might have to switch advisors.) Of course, there's always the chance that your professor is right. Maybe the question has been settled. In that event, it's back to step 1, and your reading begins again. Not to worry, though. Presumably you are gaining excellent exposure to important topics in your field. Eventually (and probably in less time than you suspect, if you use the reading method I described) you will come upon a question that is both important and needing further explanation.

3. RESEARCH TACTICS
i. Compress Your Question into Eight Words or Fewer

Once you think you've landed on the right question, my best advice is to make it as brief as possible. The reason for forcing yourself to pare down your question in this rigid manner is two-fold. First, it allows you to articulate it clearly and succinctly at the departmental cocktail party, and just as importantly on the job market. Don't underestimate the importance of those cocktail parties. When you are speaking with professors or other grad students, it makes a very good impression. People will leave that conversation thinking, "Gee, that bright grad student really knows what she's doing. I'll have to keep her in mind when I need a new research assistant. Actually, I should mention her at the faculty meeting when we rank all the grad students in our department and allocate the funding."

The second benefit of a crisp, clear question is that it enables you to keep it always in mind while you write. As you are crafting each paragraph or section of your dissertation, you can ask yourself: "Does this paragraph or section help to answer that question?" If the answer is no, then cut it out and move on to something that does. You have no time to waste. Stay on target.

At the risk of seeming gaudily self-promotional (okay, I'm guilty), here are some of my own topics, questions, and answers from books that I have written since publishing my dissertation. These should serve as further examples of how to condense your question into eight words or fewer, and how to keep your answers (theses) down to a single sentence. The thesis can be expressed in more than eight words, but I strongly recommend keeping it to one sentence.

Book Title: *Breeding Bin Ladens: America, Islam, and the Future of Europe* (Johns Hopkins University Press, 2006).

Topic: Muslim integration into European society.

Question: Why were European and American governments alienating Muslims?

Thesis: They failed to understand European Muslims' ambivalence, not antipathy, about perceived mainstream Western values.

Book Title: *Blunder: Why Smart People Make Bad Decisions* (Bloomsbury, 2008).

Topic: Decision making in international conflict.

Question: Why do people shoot themselves in the foot?

Thesis: Specific, recurrent, rigid mindsets ensnare decision makers.

Book Title: *A Sense of the Enemy: The High-Stakes History of Reading Your Rival's Mind* (Oxford University Press, 2014).

Topic: Enemy assessments in twentieth-century international conflict.

Question: What produces strategic empathy?

Thesis: One key to strategic empathy comes not from the enemy's pattern of past behavior, but from his behavior at pattern breaks.

Here's one important aspect of the questions and theses above. Each is spring-loaded. Like a coil tightly wound, each compressed question has potential energy just begging to be released. These compact questions and answers all demand elaboration. What is "strategic empathy"? What do you mean by "rigid mindsets"? What kinds of European Muslims are you talking about: immigrants or those born in Europe, young or old, Arabs or Turks or others? What does "ambivalence" really mean? What about "integration"? Your compact sentences are not just waiting for someone to ask for more explanation at a cocktail party; they are also demanding that you, the author, explain what they mean. By spring-loading your topics, questions, and theses, you are setting yourself up to fill the white space.

Initially most people struggle to condense their research question down to eight words or fewer. Remember that you will have plenty of opportunity to elaborate your question. For now, when you are just beginning the research process, force yourself to express it in this bite-sized way. You will find that it keeps you focused both in the research and the writing phases. Just as I said before that while writing, you can ask yourself if the current paragraph is helping to answer that eight-words-or-fewer question, you can also use your question nugget while conducting research. As you read through documents, diaries, studies, or any written records, you can ask if what you are reading can help to answer your question. If not, drop it and move along to something that might. Of course, you won't always know immediately if a particular record is relevant, but you will want to determine this fairly soon, before you waste hours of your day (and life) reading works that just don't matter to you at this moment. And only one thing should matter while you are in school: getting out of school with your degree in hand, and getting it with the minimum amount of years, debt, and emotional anguish. If you keep your eight-words-or-fewer question always in mind, you can target your research and writing with laserlike intensity.

2. Questions Can Be Familiar, Answers Must Be Original

As you know, the bar for a doctoral dissertation is substantially higher than for a master's thesis. A master's thesis typically needs to demonstrate mastery of a subject: meaning that you know the relevant literature on a topic and that you have analyzed a particular problem in the field. Of course the standards will vary among departments and among universities, but the expectation of originality is never as high as it is for a dissertation. In order to earn a PhD, you must make an original contribution to our understanding of a problem.

In my field, history, originality takes three principal forms. We can discover or tap new sources, devise new interpretations, or debunk old explanations. With luck, a dissertation does all three. In other humanities and social sciences the originality requirement is similar, but with little emphasis on discovering or tapping new sources. Whatever the field, the candidate is expected to tell us something we didn't know before—and be right.

Because the originality requirement seems so daunting, many grad students gravitate toward the obscure. By focusing on a subject so arcane as to be virtually unexplored, they are bound to say something that no one has previously discussed. The problem is that they choose topics not only arcane but also irrelevant. Imagine a dissertation on an analysis of the 1853 Swedish by-elections in Lower Schmorgeschburg, with special focus on precincts 8 and 9. Given that no one has ever explored this subject, you can't lose. But who the heck cares? Unless something crucial occurred in these by-elections, and unless precincts 8 and 9 were pivotal in that event, then why should anyone ever read this dissertation? How will it truly advance our understanding in any meaningful manner? Chances are that the only thing the dissertation committee members can do with this tome is cure their insomnia.

Never relegate yourself into irrelevance by studying the obscure. Always link your question to something larger—meaning something truly significant. This will not only help keep you going when the process gets toughest, it will also help you make a compelling pitch on the job market, whether you are seeking academic jobs or not.

3. Link Your Question to Something Larger

Imagine that you were actually opening your research paper, master's thesis, or PhD dissertation with an eight-word-or-fewer question. What next? The typical next sentence might begin with the words "More specifically ...," and you would elaborate and explain your question, making it more nuanced and narrow. For example, after the question, "How did Hitler make decisions?" you might write, "More specifically, how did Hitler's government make foreign policy decisions in the prewar period, 1933–1939?" And then you might explain what precisely you plan to investigate, why it is important to do so (meaning how your study advances our understanding of the subject), and then link your question to a larger puzzle. Maybe this study can provide insight into other aspects of the Nazi regime. Or perhaps it can help us understand decision making in other comparable dictatorships (if any could be comparable). The point is that you must always be able to show why your narrow little study matters. We call this the "so what?" question, and it is as crucial that you can explain it to others as it is for you to explain it to yourself.

If you cannot say why your investigation really matters, if you cannot link your question to a larger puzzle, then I suggest you drop it immediately and find something that truly matters. There are, of course, two main exceptions. If you are independently wealthy with no need of finding future employment, then by all means, knock yourself out and write about whatever the heck you please. You might, if you're feeling particularly magnanimous at the time, donate a building or two to your university. I assure you that you'll be handed, uhhh, I mean you will have earned, whatever degree you desire. Alternatively, you might simply be obsessed with a question that matters only to you. Perhaps you are willing to say, "Let the consequences be damned. Gosh darn it, I don't give a bleep if I'm oodles in debt and can't find a job. Darn it, I'll have my answer to sustain me!" If that is the case, then you should pursue your irrelevant question as though it were the

Maltese Falcon. And if a sinister fat man and creepy thin man with an ill-defined Eastern European accent should wind up chasing you across the world to obtain your thesis once you find it, well then, it will certainly be an exciting quest. Maybe they'll even make a movie about it.[2] But, my friends, if you are like most of us and either need/want a job, or need/want to devote several years of your life to something that actually advances human understanding, I suggest you link your question to a larger puzzle.

There are two simple ways to approach this. You can either start with a narrow question of interest to you and figure out how it will advance our understanding of a bigger puzzle, or you can begin with a big, unsolved puzzle in your field and figure out how to tackle one small piece of it. In the method for finding a research question that I described above, you would be starting with the big puzzle and determining which aspects had not been adequately addressed. In the example I gave of urban crime, the question was why it persists at high rates, and you identified the various types of answers that sociologists have given. Then you looked for your own angle into the puzzle: the systemic pressures of the justice system. Starting with the big unsolved puzzles is probably the better way to begin, if you have had little exposure to a field. Your freshness, in fact your ignorance, is a huge advantage. It enables you to approach old problems with what Zen Buddhists call a "beginner's mind." You will not be encumbered by years of stale thinking. You can more readily question the things that the experts have taken for granted. Who knew that ignorance could be such bliss?

---

2. In case you are puzzled by these last few sentences, they are a reference to the classic film *The Maltese Falcon*. If you haven't seen it, it's the stuff that dreams are made of.

As for the other approach—starting with a narrow question of interest to you and determining how to link it to a bigger puzzle—this method can also be effective, but you will need to get honest feedback from the experts. Remember step 1 in the five-step question-finding process: ask the experts. If you adopt this approach, you'll need to ask them if your question is truly significant, worthy of investigation. Again, your advisors might be wrong. They might dismiss your question by saying that it has already been answered. And then you'll need to determine if they're right by scrutinizing the conventional wisdom. Whichever approach you take to finding a question, you must be certain that you do not know the answer.

4. Let Your Questions Guide Your Research

This small section is important for anyone doing archival research. If that is not you, just skip ahead to section 5.

The first problem you'll encounter in any archive is volume. No, not that it's too noisy in there. Most likely you'll only hear the clackety-clack of keyboards and the faux shutter sounds of iPhone cameras. The problem is with the volume of records. There's just too much, and you'll want to read it all. This desire stems in part from a natural and altogether admirable intellectual curiosity, and in part from sheer terror: "What if I miss something crucial?" And that's when the anxiety dreams begin. You see yourself at a lectern, formally dressed, confidently delivering your pathbreaking, field-changing, career-propelling findings to a room of riveted experts, when suddenly a man in a bow tie with a pocket protector leaps up from the audience and exclaims, "Excuse me, but haven't you overlooked the McGuffin Files, which clearly undermine your entire thesis?" You stagger backward in horror. If you had only looked at that one last set of papers before you left the archives.

I suppose this nightmare vision is possible, but it is also highly unlikely, assuming you have consulted the great majority of the records most relevant to your narrow question. You have also thoroughly gutted the secondary literature on your subject, so you know what the field knows, and you know what sources it has drawn on. If Professor Pocket Protector is aware of the McGuffin Files, you probably are, too, because they would have already been discussed in the literature. And if your mentors are of any use at all, they would have alerted you to these files long before you ever published anything. All this is to say that your task in the archives is not to try to read everything, because you can't. If you try, you'll get nowhere. You'll drown in an ocean of records. Instead, your task is to identify those records of greatest relevance to your question, the ones most likely to help you solve your riddle.

When you walk into any archive, you are guided by your questions. You cannot afford to flounder about aimlessly, dipping in and out of every set of records that seems remotely interesting. Instead you must ask one question of each set of records listed in the catalogues: how likely are these records to help answer my research question? You can divide them into three groups: most likely to answer your question, somewhat likely, and least likely. If you manage to consume all of the records in the first category of "most likely," consider yourself blessed. Given the enormous volume of material, be selective. If you can restrict yourself to focusing first on those records in the most-likely category, you will greatly enhance your efficiency. Remember, it's not so easy to visit an archive more than once during your dissertation research phase. There's a good chance that you might not be able to return. Make the most of your time there by letting your questions choose your records.

There is another benefit to keeping your research questions firmly in view as you read archival records. When you know what you are looking for, you also know what to skip. In order to maximize your time, you will need to do a tremendous amount of skipping. If you encounter a document that seems unlikely even to address your research question, send it back and order up more. Don't be hesitant to jettison the inappropriate. ("Jettison the inappropriate" is also how my friend described her decision to divorce her husband, but that's a separate story.)

As with almost every rule, there are exceptions. One crucial caveat is this: if you discover some exciting batch of documents that do not relate to your question but which could make for a fascinating dissertation, you might consider changing your question. Many great books emerge from unexpected finds. If you are lucky enough to unearth such a treasure, consult your doctor or pharmacist before taking Xanax to settle your nerves, and then consult your advisor for advice. Sources do have a funny way of guiding your research. Almost no one ends up writing the dissertation she began with. Questions evolve as you learn more about your subject, and questions also evolve as you encounter new sources. Years ago I had an undergraduate advisor tell me that a truly good research project directs you, rather than you directing it. He meant that the sources take you in directions you cannot anticipate, and you need to follow their leads. This advice can seem completely contradictory to the advice I've just been giving: that you should let your questions guide your research. Here's how to make sense of it. Your questions do drive your research, but the sources can cause you to alter your question. The point is to start out with questions in mind rather than plopping down in an archive, ordering random collections of records, and seeing what's out there. If you start with clear questions, you will be much more efficient. And if, in the process of reading the relevant records you discover sources that yield new questions, you might choose to pursue those new questions. I would caution you, however, to think through carefully whether these new questions are likely to result in a dissertation superior to the one based on your original question.

5. Never Draw Your Conclusions
Before Doing the Research

Frequently, and more frequently than you might believe, I have students (and sometimes even other scholars) tell me that they want to write on X, because they want to show that Y. In other words, they have already decided that they know the answer to their question *before* even taking the first step in conducting the research. This means that they are not truly interested in learning the answer. Instead, they simply want to tell others what to believe. Folks, listen up. This is not scholarship. This is rhetoric. And if that's what you want to do, then you should quit school and join either a disreputable DC think tank, or work for Fox News. (Yes, I know, the liberal news shows are just as bad: unfair and unbalanced.) Never forget what business you are in. Entrepreneurs are in the business of making money. Athletes are in the business of winning games. And scholars are in the business of seeking truth. We don't always get there. Often we get it wrong. But the aim is that through our collective efforts, inch by inch, we will grope our way toward the truth. We will discover the causes and cures of diseases. We will learn why some countries are rich while others are poor, and possibly how to correct this. We will understand the causes and consequences of historic events and learn why they unfolded as they did. Each field has its overarching aims, and all scholarship is devoted to achieving them through the pursuit of truth. Sounds grandiose? It is. And it is entirely worth doing. If you choose to be part of that collective effort, even if only while in school, you must begin with an open mind. For the surest sign of a limited intellect is a closed mind.

Here's a depressing story. I once gave an hour-long lecture to more than one thousand grad students about how to do research. I worked on this talk for weeks. I had jokes, surprises, tension, and carefully constructed explanations for how to begin a project. The audience seemed to love it. They laughed at the right places, asked thoughtful questions, and responded intelligently when I engaged them directly. One of the three main points I made about research was to *never draw your conclusions before you begin.* The next day one of those students came to my office to say how much he enjoyed my lecture and to ask if I would consider being his thesis advisor. When I asked what he wanted to write on, he said, "Well I want to show that . . ." and he described a project for which he had already determined the result before having done a lick of research. Friends, there are few things more deflating to a teacher than to be seated across from living proof of your abject failure.

Actually, if I may digress, this reminds me of a wedding speech I once gave for my childhood friend Peter. I spent twenty minutes telling funny stories about the groom as a little boy. I shared heartwarming tales of our youthful antics together. And I detailed some of our most meaningful moments of friendship over the decades. The crowd seemed to be eating it up. And not long after it was all over and the applause died down, I passed an enthusiastic lady who reached out and warmly clutched my arm. "That was such a lovely, touching speech you gave. I was truly moved. Thank you so much for that," she beamed. I was all smiles until she added, "So how do you know Peter?"

Lesson learned: you can't teach all the people all the time. But I hope I can teach you this crucial concept. If you only want to prove a point, then you are not genuinely interested in answering your question. So why bother? Both the process and the product of your dissertation will be rather boring. On the other hand, the most interesting theses are the ones where you honestly don't know the answer and you are surprised by what you discover. Those are the most compelling works to write as well as read. So please keep an open mind about your question. And this brings me to my next bit of advice.

6. Confront Counterevidence Directly

Malcolm Gladwell is arguably one of the most accomplished narrative nonfiction writers of our time. Yet scholars are quick to deprecate his work. They forget that he has done a tremendous amount to stimulate interest in social science. His books have even made a few scholars famous and rich. In 2013, when Gladwell published *David and Goliath,* social scientists jumped all over him, writing highly critical reviews and commentaries against the arguments in that book. It seemed as though they couldn't wait to stomp on the goose who had just laid a golden egg. Believe it or not, their stomping is of direct relevance to you.

Many scholars insisted that Gladwell cherry-picked his evidence. He allegedly failed to confront counterevidence directly. In various interviews, Gladwell offered a variety of defenses. At one point he said: "If my books appear to a reader to be oversimplified, then you shouldn't read them: you're not the audience!"[3] Please do not use this defense when speaking with your advisor, if for no other reason than that your advisor is forced to read what you write. In another interview Gladwell admitted that he had selected the evidence that best supported his claims, but he defended his actions by saying, essentially, that everybody does it.

> You know when you make an argument, we evaluate the evidence and then we choose the evidence we feel is the most, uh, significant. And that's what I'm doing in my books and I, you know, there are people who make arguments that maybe I've chosen the wrong evidence. That's fine. I don't think that—but I don't think I'm, I should be singled out as the only person in the world who selects from a lot of different arguments the ones that he finds most persuasive. I think that's what human beings do, isn't it?[4]

It was an unfortunate comment.

What Gladwell said is perhaps true of many people, including lawyers in a courtroom, whose job is to defend their client's life. The litigator must make the best of a bad situation. She must present the evidence that shows her client in the best possible light while simultaneously downplaying the evidence that reflects poorly on him. In very sharp contrast, the scholar's job is to seek the truth. When you write, you are not drafting a legal brief, hoping to persuade others of something that may or may not be true. The lawyer is not paid to determine her client's innocence or guilt; she is simply there to defend him. (By the way, it's not clear to me why someone's life should hinge on the rhetorical skill of one's

3. Oliver Burkeman, "Malcolm Gladwell: 'If my books appear oversimplified, then you shouldn't read them,'" *The Guardian*, September 29, 2013.

4. Malcolm Gladwell, interview with Jeremy Hobson, "Here and Now," WBUR Boston, National Public Radio, October 15, 2013. http://hereandnow.wbur.org/2013/10/15/gladwell-david-goliath.

attorney, but fairness is not the hallmark of most justice systems.) The scholar, on the other hand, must first gather and weigh the evidence, and then decide where the truth lies. Only then do you lay out your case in the clearest and most persuasive manner possible. You are more judge than lawyer. You must fairly and critically assess all plausible explanations. You do not ignore counterevidence. If that counterevidence undermines or disproves your conclusion, then you change your conclusion. If one study offers evidence in support of your initial hypothesis, but ninety-nine other studies suggest the opposite, you had better not fail to mention the other ninety-nine. Instead, you must either modify your conclusion or explain why the ninety-nine other studies are wrong. This can happen, of course. Sometimes the 99 percent get it wrong, often because they have based their studies on the same flawed assumptions, and one person comes along, corrects for that error, and winds up with an entirely different result. If that is the case, then say so and prove it. Otherwise, don't rest your case on the one outlying study that just happens to support the conclusion that you wish to prove, because that, my friends, is a quick ticket to a short career. Well, I suppose I should say it's a ticket to a short *academic* career. Alternatively, if you want to have a phenomenally successful career as a bestselling journalist who writes about social science, if you want to make millions of dollars and be paid staggering sums to give talks around the world, then maybe cherry-picking is the way to go. (Hmmm … can someone remind me why I went into academia? What the hell was I thinking?)

7. Make a Clear and Convincing Case

Now that we're clear on how lawyers differ from scholars, I hope I can safely borrow some legal terminology without causing confusion. In lawyers' defense, they do employ standards of evidence, and we can use these standards as a rough guide to the degree of proof you would like to obtain. But remember that your goal is first to determine the truth, based on a careful weighing of evidence, and only then is it to build your case with words. As you approach the evidence you gathered, you are trying to determine what it all means. So in order to figure that out, you will need to challenge each plausible hypothesis. You will therefore need some standard by which to measure the strength of each case.

Imagine a murder trial in which a victim was found dead in her home. The lowest level of proof is called "circumstantial." That's where you have evidence, but the evidence is rather flimsy. It could be used to show something very different from what the chief prosecutor is trying to prove. Just because a glove belonging to the accused was found at the crime scene doesn't prove that the accused person committed the crime. He might have dropped it earlier that day when he came by to deliver flowers, as he claims. In contrast to circumstantial evidence, the highest level of proof is called "beyond reasonable doubt." That's where the accused's glove is splattered with the victim's blood, it contains gunpowder residue from the pistol that shot the victim, and the surveillance camera clearly shows the accused shooting the deceased. (Hmmm ... let Alan Dershowitz try to argue his way around that!) When you weigh your evidence, you will almost never achieve "beyond reasonable doubt." That bar is too high for most humanities and social science dissertations. But you also cannot rely on circumstantial evidence. That's not good enough. Instead, you need a level of proof as close to "beyond reasonable doubt" as you can get. We call that level "clear and convincing." Achieving that level of certainty should be your aim. Get above "circumstantial" and as close as you reasonably can to "beyond reasonable doubt."[5]

THE RECAP

- Know the difference between your topic, your question, and your answer.
- Articulate each in a single, crisp, clear sentence.
- Know that questions are meant to fill gaps in our understanding.
- Use the five-step process to find your question.
- Compress your question into eight words or fewer.
- Link your question to something larger.
- Never draw your conclusions before doing the research.
- Let your questions guide your sources.
- Confront counterevidence directly.
- Make a clear and convincing case.

If you train yourself to do only these basic things, you will be far ahead of many of your peers—and even of some scholars. I'm sure you realize that there is far more to conducting high-quality research than just these things. My aim is to give you the most essential elements to get you on the proper footing. The rest you will have to learn from other scholars, from books, and by trial and error—though I hope your experience will be neither a trial nor full of error. Keep the guidance I have given in mind, and you will greatly enhance your chance to succeed. Good luck.

---

5. I have simplified the legal terminology regarding evidence. For a more thorough explanation of categories of evidence, consult a practicing attorney, but remember that he'll bill you by the minute, so make him talk fast.

Oh, and one more thing. Do you remember that advice I slipped in earlier about bringing passion to the page? If you forget everything else, just remember that one idea. Because if your research feels like a tiresome chore, something is seriously wrong. Conducting research won't be sidesplitting hilarity every moment, but the majority of the time you should be engaged by your questions, excited by the process, and eager to find the answers. I'll confess to an embarrassing secret about me. Each time I've neared the end of writing a book, I am gripped by a very silly thought. I find myself praying to God (and I'm not typically a prayerful person) that I won't be hit by a bus before I finish. Naturally, I hope not to be hit by a bus even when I'm not finishing a book, but I'm especially vigilant at these times. I feel that the world must know the answer to the questions I've been exploring, and I have to get this information out there. In my rational brain I realize how absurd this is, and yet I delude myself into believing that others might care as much about my project as I do. And maybe someone, somewhere, just might. This is the kind of drive that should power your research. You should be excited by the quest. You should truly love reading, writing, speaking, and thinking about your question. And you should yearn, yes yearn, to discover an important truth.

CPSIA information can be obtained
at www.ICGtesting.com
Printed in the USA
BVHW031320210721
612545BV00004B/99